Maple and Vine

by Jordan Harrison

A SAMUEL FRENCH ACTING EDITION

FOUNDED 1830

SAMUELFRENCH.COM

ISBN 978-0-573-70021-7   Printed in U.S.A.   #28063

MUSIC USE NOTE

MAPLE AND VINE premiered at the Humana Festival of New American Plays in March 2011. The production was directed by Anne Kauffman, with scenic design by Brian Sidney Bembridge, costume design by Connie Furr Soloman, lighting design by Jeff Nellis, sound design by Benjamin Marcum, and properties design by Alice Baldwin. The stage manager was Melissa Rae Miller. The dramaturg was Amy Wegener. The directing assistant was Rachel Paul, and the production assistant was Nick Bussett. The cast was as follows:

KATHA	Kate Turnbull
RYU	Peter Kim
DEAN	Paul Niebanck
ELLEN/JENNA	Jeanine Serralles
ROGER/OMAR	Jesse Pennington

MAPLE AND VINE had its New York premiere at Playwrights Horizons in December 2011 under the direction of Anne Kauffman. The production had scenic design by Alexander Dodge, costume design by Ilona Somogyi, lighting design by David Weiner, and properties design by Jessica Provenzale. The original music and sound design was by Bray Poor. The stage manager was William H. Lang. The assistant stage manager was Ryan Gohsman, and the directing assistant was Ilana Becker. The cast was as follows:

KATHA	Marin Ireland
RYU	Peter Kim
DEAN	Trent Dawson
ELLEN/JENNA	Jeanine Serralles
ROGER/OMAR	Pedro Pascal

CHARACTERS

KATHA – mid to late 30s.

RYU – mid to late 30s.

DEAN – late 30s.

ELLEN – late 30s. Also plays **JENNA**.

ROGER – mid to late 30s. Also plays **OMAR**.

PRODUCTION NOTES

This is a play with many locations. The productions I've been involved with, while scenically ambitious, benefited from reducing the number of locations in the interest of fluidity. At the same time, many locations were minimally suggested. This is all to say, if your theater (like most theaters) isn't graced with lightning-quick hydraulic lifts or automated platforms as silent as a pin dropping, do not despair. I can imagine a production where costumes and wigs do nearly all the work in transporting us to the 1950s. While I can't say that locations are unimportant, I don't think they are as important as the narrative momentum. In this play, the way one scene "talks" to the following scene is sometimes as important as what happens within the scenes themselves.

In Part One, Dean and Ellen are speaking to a group of people who have already made the decision to try out the SDO but have not moved there yet. Think of it as a kind of large-scale orientation meeting.

SCRIPT NOTE

A slash mark (/) indicates overlapping dialogue.

PART ONE

1.

(In the darkness, we hear:
Sounds of a rainforest.)

(The rainforest stops abruptly, and we hear:
Sounds of an ocean.)

(The ocean stops abruptly, and we hear:
Sounds of a babbling brook.)

(And back to the rainforest.)

RYU. Make up your mind.

(As our eyes adjust, we can make out **KATHA** *and* **RYU** *in bed.)*

KATHA. I've been awake for two hours.

RYU. Oh Baby.

KATHA. I've been counting the seconds between the jungle insects. There's a pattern. *(talking along with the sounds:)* Chirp-chirp. *(pause)* Chirp-chirp. Then it gets longer. You don't care.

RYU. I know what you're going to say, but what if you took a pill.

KATHA. I don't want to be zonked out all of tomorrow.

(Pause. She listens to **RYU** *breathing. We hear a* **WOMAN**'s *strident voice from the street below.)*

WOMAN IN THE STREET. Simon. I know you're up there.

KATHA. Oh no.

WOMAN. Simon buzz me in.

Why are you DOING THIS TO ME?

KATHA. She's back.

RYU. Who?

KATHA. She usually comes around 2.

WOMAN. Why are you DOING THIS TO ME?

> (**RYU** *presses a button on the alarm clock and blue glowing numbers read "2:03."*)

RYU. She's right on time.

KATHA. It isn't funny.
This is, like, the farthest
I'll ever get from being
at work. This is it.
I should be having a
dream, / I should be   **WOMAN.** *(overlapping at"/")* I
somewhere else, but   came all this way, I took
instead I'm just – here.   THREE TRAINS so I
                                            don't see how you can be
                                            DOING THIS TO ME!

RYU. Jesus.

                                  WOMAN. No one deserves this
                                        Simon.

KATHA. No, Simon. No one
deserves this.

> (**KATHA** *continues in a clenched, terrible way – stoked by the voice outside.*)

KATHA. I lie here all night
thinking about the
whole day in front
of me I write imagi-   **WOMAN.** Simon, if I have to
nary emails I make   stand out here in the
imaginary trips to the   cold any longer I think
copy room so when I   I'm really going to LOSE
actually LIVE IT it's   IT.
like I'm doing it all
over again like like
Sisyphus or like Hell, I

think it's probably very much what Hell would be like, this kind of cold like repetition with no chance of – peace.

RYU. Baby please – You're shaking.

WOMAN. Simon!

RYU. Who's Simon?

KATHA. Who knows.

RYU. Is he the one with the pug?

KATHA. It's not like I've ever seen our neighbors.

WOMAN. SIMON!

KATHA. And yet I feel like I know him.

RYU. Baby, how about a pill.

KATHA. You're always trying to medicate me.

RYU. I'm always trying to help you. It's been six months.

KATHA. It takes as long as it takes.

RYU. Of course.

(Short pause)

KATHA. What if this is *me* now.

RYU. No.

KATHA. Hold me for a while?

RYU. Sure. I can do that.

(He holds her. **KATHA** *starts to suck her thumb. It helps, a little.)*

WOMAN. Simon!

2.

(**DEAN** *speaks out to us. He wears an immaculate 1950s suit and well-shined wing tips. He takes off his hat, politely, before speaking. Revealing slick, aggressively parted hair.*)

(**ELLEN** *stands further off, almost out of the light. She wears a smart, feminine suit, with hat and gloves.*)

DEAN. First of all, welcome. Welcome to the SDO.

I bet you're all feeling pretty anxious.

"Am I going to use the right words."

"Am I going to walk the right way."

I mean gosh, you've just taken a pretty huge step, right?

The first thing to remember is that all of us were newcomers at one point.

The other thing to remember – and this one really helped me – the other thing to remember is that the 1950s *weren't in black and white*. It sounds silly, but it's easy to think like that. All we've seen are the photographs. Old TV shows. But people in the '50s had yellow shirts and red sneakers just like you and me. So the main thing to remember is that you can live in color. You don't have to go around trying to act like someone in an old photo. I mean anyway you can't, because they're a photo, and you're…you.

That's what this place is for. So you can feel like you again.

I'm sure you all have a lot of questions.

"What do I wear?" "How do I talk?"

"How do I explain this to the kids?"

Ellen and I will help you answer all of these perfectly normal questions.

Everyone, this is my lovely wife Ellen.

ELLEN. Hello everyone.

DEAN. Isn't she something?

3.

(KATHA and RYU's apartment, the next morning. KATHA sits slumped in pajamas, staring at her laptop computer. Maybe she's still in bed. A bowl of cereal sits beside her, untouched. She looks happy in a tranquilized sort of way. RYU is fully dressed. He's also looking at a laptop, but more actively – web surfing, sipping his coffee.)

(We hear period-sounding voices from Katha's computer:)

MALE VOICE. Don't you like it?

FEMALE VOICE. Like it?

(Soaring music plays.)

It's more exquisite than any dress I could ever have imagined.

MALE VOICE. Puff sleeves.

FEMALE VOICE. The puffiest in the world. You are a man of impeccable taste, Matthew.

KATHA. So beautiful…

MALE VOICE. Well, you don't / want to get your dress dirty.

RYU. What?

KATHA. *(still watching the video, rapt)* Just, the way Matthew doesn't ever say "I love you" but you just *know*?

RYU. Who's Matthew?

KATHA. Oh, sorry. It's "Anne of Green Gables."

RYU. Didn't you already watch that?

KATHA. There are 26 installments.

(sheepish)

The things they have on YouTube.

RYU. The things people look for on YouTube.

KATHA. It's my childhood. Don't begrudge me my opiates.

RYU. I never begrudge your opiates.

(He walks out of the room.)

KATHA. It's a nostalgia thing. But I'm not sure whether it's nostalgia for the 1880s or the *19*80s. My mother and I watched it all together on TV.

(**RYU** *comes back in brushing his teeth.*)

It always seemed like a nice life. Go to the one-room schoolhouse. Do arithmetic on your slate. Dip some girl's pigtails in the inkwell.

(**RYU** *disappears into the bathroom to spit.*)

It seemed like a nice life.

RYU. *(off)* I was just googling? There are some really affordable places in Nyack.

KATHA. Nyack?

(*He comes back in.*)

RYU. It'd be quieter, we'd have space. It's just the commute.

(*She hits pause. The music stops.*)

KATHA. Space for what.

RYU. You know, space.

KATHA. *(thin ice)* Space for kids?

RYU. Space for whatever.

KATHA. Let's – not have this conversation now.

RYU. Why not?

KATHA. I'm getting ready for work.

RYU. You don't look like you're getting ready. You look like you're at a slumber party.

KATHA. I'm eating breakfast.

(*She grabs her cereal bowl. She starts the video again. Soaring music from the computer.* **RYU** *shakes his head. He starts to put on his coat.*)

RYU. Well, see you tonight.

KATHA. *(not looking up)* Okay.

I'm home pretty late.

(**RYU***'s hand on the doorknob.*)

What's your day like?

(**RYU** *starts to cry.*)

KATHA. *(cont.)* Oh. Oh no. *(She hits pause.)*
What'd I say?

RYU. *(through tears)* It's just – it's like every day. I'll get *through* it. And then I come home, and you're –. There isn't any –

KATHA. Here. Come here.

RYU. I'm the one who's supposed to be there for you.

KATHA. There aren't any rules.

4.

*(**DEAN** speaks directly to us.)*

DEAN. It wasn't that the modern world was too fast, or too noisy. In a way, it was too *quiet*. Let me explain. In the 21st century, everything's pretty easy, right? You have your drive-thru espresso. Your drive-thru pharmacy. Or why go to the store when you can get it online? You hardly have to interact with anyone – except for all those people you've never even met who enter your life through your computer, pulling you every which way.

In the '50s it's different. In the '50s you have to *go* places. You have to *talk* to people. You pick up the phone to make a call and there's an operator on the other end and you say "Good morning." Or say you want to find something out, you go down to the library and Miss Wilkes looks it up in the Dewey Decimals. There's a separate store for meat, and fish, and fruit, and a gent behind each counter who knows your name. A man brings the milk every morning.

In the modern world, I used to make it through half the day without talking to a single soul. I used to have it so easy. And now, looking back – I realize how lonely I was.

5.

(At the office, late that morning. **KATHA** *stares at her phone, catatonic.)*

*(***OMAR** *and* **JENNA** *watch her from a distance.)*

OMAR. Pssst.

JENNA. What's going on?

OMAR. Haven't you noticed?

JENNA. *(nodding)* She should really rethink the sweater.

OMAR. No, I mean – she hasn't moved in like ten minutes.

JENNA. Why not?

OMAR. 'Cause she's depressed I guess.

JENNA. What about?

OMAR. Nothing.

JENNA. How do you know it's nothing?

OMAR. Her husband's a doctor.

JENNA. What kind?

OMAR. Plastic surgeon.

*(***KATHA** *appears to be giving herself a private little pep talk. Maybe she gives herself a light slap on each cheek.)*

JENNA. Ohmygod.

OMAR. What's she doing?

JENNA. Ohmygod.

*(***KATHA** *picks up the receiver.)*

OMAR. Every day she comes in later.

JENNA. I know, isn't it great?

OMAR. No, I mean: What if they let her go?

JENNA. Let her go. I'll take her job.

OMAR. *(loving it)* Don't be terrible! Besides, you wouldn't get it.

JENNA. Why not?

OMAR. You're too nice.

JENNA. I know, I'm nice right?

OMAR. You're *too* nice.

In that job you have to be able to tell people / No.

KATHA. *(overlapping with* **OMAR**'s *"No")* No! I will not hold!

(She has been put on hold. She hangs up, starts to dial again.)

JENNA. And I suppose you can tell people No?

OMAR. *(arch)* Maybe.

*(***OMAR** *starts to leave.)*

JENNA. Fancy salad place for lunch?

OMAR. Always.

(And he's gone, headed towards **KATHA***'s office.)*

KATHA. *(brightly)* Yes, you just put me on hold? Do not do that again.

–

Marcus please.

–

Katha at Random House.

–

Well I'm pretty sure he's at his desk for *me* because he left me three messages about the Labradoodle book.

–

An early *lunch,* what a luxury. You'd think the man putting together the most urgent coffee table book of our times wouldn't have time to –

–

No. I'll be here.

*(***KATHA** *hangs up. She stares at her phone.)*

I'll be here.

*(***KATHA** *sucks her thumb unconsciously.* **OMAR** *comes sidling up to the doorway.)*

OMAR. Katha? Knock knock.

KATHA. Who's there?

OMAR. Omar.

KATHA. Omar who.

OMAR. *(concerned)* You know, *Omar.*

Oh, I get it – we're doing a thing, a knock-knock thing.

(Short pause)

KATHA. You know for a homosexual you're not very funny.

OMAR. Well, you're my boss, so.

KATHA. So.

OMAR. So we don't really have that relationship?

(Beat)

Are you ready?

KATHA. Ready…

OMAR. You have the Department Head meeting in ten minutes.

*(For a moment, **KATHA** seems to forget how to breathe.)*

Unless you want me to tell them you're busy sucking your thumb.

(He exits.)

KATHA. "Unless you want me to tell them…"

That's good. Maybe he is funny.

You're talking out loud.

(She stares at her phone. Inhales and exhales. She picks up the receiver and dials just two numbers.)

Yes. Put me through to Human Resources.

6.

(ELLEN speaks directly to us. DEAN stands farther off now.)

ELLEN. In the beginning, most people try a little too hard with the lingo.

It's easy to get carried away. There are lots of fun terms: "Don't be a square." "Back-seat bingo."

But you don't want to use them all in one sentence.

DEAN. "Hey cat, don't be a square, how 'bout we jump in my hot rod and play a little back-seat bingo?"

ELLEN. I'm not that kind of girl!

DEAN. Oh yes you are.

(They have a laugh at this.)

ELLEN. *(to us again)* That was a lot of fun. But you see the problem. You can end up sounding like you're a person at a theme party, not a person. The most colorful slang from the '50s comes from the Beats and the Hotrodders, so nice ordinary people will want to use those words sparingly.

DEAN. What people don't realize is that a lot of the most common '50s sayings are still in use in 2011, so they'll come naturally to you.

"Cool it." "Make out." "Have a blast."

"Word from the bird."

Just kidding. I was just making sure you were paying attention.

ELLEN. Oh Dean.

Sometimes you just razz my berries.

7.

(Early that afternoon. **KATHA** *and* **RYU** *in Madison Square Park, with hot dogs.* **KATHA** *isn't eating hers.* **RYU** *still has his scrubs on.)*

KATHA. Happy? I don't know.

RYU. I mean the last time you really – felt like yourself.

KATHA. I guess when we rented bikes in Amsterdam? And we got falafel?

*(***RYU***'s beeper beeps. He takes it out.)*

That was almost two years ago.

RYU. *(glancing at it)* What about Cape Cod – was that after? When we pulled the bikes over

KATHA. And we had oysters from that stand.

RYU. That was good.

(Beat)

KATHA. So the secret is bikes.

RYU. Or food.

(He takes a bite of his hot dog, trying to be jaunty.)

KATHA. Great, Ryu.

Then we're all set, we'll just get some…*bikes* / and and

RYU. Baby.

KATHA. and some hot dogs and some Cherry fucking / *Garcia*

RYU. Baby okay / okay

KATHA. and it'll be like it never happened!

RYU. Of course it happened. It was terrible. But that doesn't mean we have to give up.

KATHA. Oh right, "Snap out of it, Katha – it's been six whole months, get over it. / Chin up, kiddo."

RYU. I didn't say that. I would never / say that.

KATHA. "Six months, time to pop out another one!"

RYU. Now you're just / being crazy –

KATHA. Maybe I don't want to love something for all that time again just to have it, to have it / stolen away!

RYU. Settle down.

KATHA. We saw him, Ryu! We saw him!

(quieter now, spent)

He was real.

RYU. Of course he was.

He was mine too.

KATHA. I'm sorry – shit.

You must get / tired of this routine.

RYU. Don't be sorry.

KATHA. I love you.

RYU. I love you.

KATHA. I want us to be happy.

RYU. I think…people aren't happy. People have *never* been happy. The whole idea is a tyranny. Slaves building the pyramids…*Serfs.* They didn't have enough time to ask "Am I happy?" This is not even a hundred-year-old idea: "Am I happy."

KATHA. Maybe that's what happy *is.*

RYU. What.

KATHA. Not having enough time to wonder if you're happy.

*(**RYU***'s beeper beeps again.)*

RYU. No, that's just busy.

(He looks at it.)

I should, I'm sorry –

(He stands up, brushes crumbs off his pants.)

We'll keep talking tonight.

KATHA. You just got here.

RYU. You think it stops?

KATHA. I know

RYU. Bags of blood, and bags of *fat…*

KATHA. *("tasty")* Mmm

RYU. …and 15-year-olds who want boobs.
I have to go back. You do too.

KATHA. No I don't. I quit.

(**RYU** *takes her in – she is strangely cavalier.*)

RYU. You quit?

KATHA. I quit. Finito Mussolini.

RYU. When?

KATHA. This morning.

RYU. Why didn't you say that before?

KATHA. I didn't feel like talking about it.

(*Pause.* **RYU** *is deeply weirded out.*)

(*His phone rings.*)

RYU. Jesus. (*The phone rings.*)
I'm going to cancel my procedures. I mean you're clearly – (*The phone rings.*)
Are you sure you're not –

KATHA. I'm not a flight risk. Go. (*The phone rings.*)

RYU. I'll be right back. (*answering*) Hello?

(**RYU** *runs off.* **KATHA** *doesn't know what to do with herself. She takes a first bite of her hot dog.*)

(**DEAN** *enters in his '50s garb. He is lost, squinting at street names. There is something unmistakably, gorgeously out of place about him.*)

DEAN. Excuse me.

KATHA. (*giving him the signal for "I just have to swallow this"*) Mmph.

DEAN. Oh, sorry.

(*He offers her the handkerchief out of his breast pocket in one smooth gesture.*)

KATHA. No, it's fine. Sorry.

DEAN. Not at all. Do you know where 200 Fifth Avenue is?

KATHA. Oh yeah, it's confusing. The entrance is on 25th. That's right by where I work. Worked.

DEAN. Well, lucky I ran into you.

(He tips his hat, starting to go.)

Thank you.

KATHA. Job interview?

DEAN. What? No. Why do you ask?

KATHA. Just, the suit and everything. It's just pretty put together.

DEAN. Thank you. I have the same one in navy and dark brown.

KATHA. This whole thing you have going – *(making a circling gesture with her hands, as if circumscribing his outfit)* – it's like something out of the '50s.

DEAN. Yes.

KATHA. Is that what they're doing downtown now? Let me guess, there's nothing shocking left so the only shocking thing is to be straight-laced. We've come full circle.

(He just looks at her.)

Or is it less… *(succumbing to self-consciousness)* self-conscious.

DEAN. I'm not part of a fashion movement. If that's what you're suggesting.

KATHA. Oh I don't mean to make it sound… / superficial.

DEAN. That's all right. We're used to people being suspicious.

KATHA. Suspicious?

DEAN. Of the way we do things. Especially people who are content with the way the world is nowadays.

KATHA. "Content."

What's that like?

(He seems to really see her for the first time.)

DEAN. What I mean is, we're used to explaining ourselves to people.

KATHA. Who's we?

DEAN. May I sit down?

8.

(**DEAN** *speaks directly to us.*)

DEAN. I'm called back, now and then, on business. Spreading the word.

And it's not just my job to tell the rest of the world about us. I have to decide what to tell *us* about *them*. I have more access to the news, and if it's gossip about so-and-so is dating so-and-so, of course I don't tell you – but when a plane crashes into the World Trade Center I tell you, when the war in Iraq starts I tell you.

Because I have more access to the outside world, it can be a struggle for me. I have a cell phone, for emergencies. I keep it in a drawer in my house. I keep the drawer locked. Just knowing it's there can be hard. It can be a distraction. That's why people today can't think straight, because there are so many distractions. They are not quiet in their mind. If you're here, you probably know that already.

It may be hard at first. I won't lie to you. When you first come to the SDO, you're used to a different kind of freedom. In the Society of Dynamic Obsolescence, there are very specific boundaries. By which I mean, if you're a gardener, you garden – you won't get invited into the house of the man you're working for. If you are a homemaker, you make your home. That's what you do. You don't start an Ultimate Frisbee team, you don't go backpacking in Thailand. Your husband and kids are going to be home soon and dinner has to be on the table. You are not free. But in another way, you're more free.

We may seem behind bars to them, but to us, they are behind the bars.

9.

(KATHA and RYU returning to their apartment, early that evening.)

RYU. I thought you were like college friends. I never imagined you'd befriended this – strange clean man who speaks in complete sentences.

KATHA. Didn't you like him?

RYU. I didn't like that he was trying to sell us something.

KATHA. He wasn't *selling* something. He was explaining his way of life.

How long has it been since we met someone who seemed so...

RYU. Don't say happy.

KATHA. He can't be much older than us. He was us a few years ago.

RYU. So he said.

KATHA. And now there he is with his briefcase and his little hat, he's got it all figured out.

But it's silly, right?

RYU. It's not just silly. It's a cult.

KATHA. It's not a cult. They have non-profit status.

RYU. I'm not sure I even get it. It's like Civil War reenactors?

KATHA. Except for you live there.

RYU. Crazy.

KATHA. But I think the intriguing part is when you hear 1950s you think it's going to be all *Stepford Wives*. You think identical houses, identical cars, a kid on each lawn all bouncing their balls in unison. But it's not that. It's not just suburbs. There's a whole universe in there.

RYU. Did you just call it intriguing?

KATHA. You can be anything there. Beat poets. Secret Communists. They need dissenters too, you heard him. We wouldn't have to be June Cleaver and...her husband, help me

RYU. Ward

KATHA. Ward Cleaver.

RYU. You said, "We."

KATHA. What?

RYU. "We" wouldn't have to be June –

KATHA. Oh, I mean "we" like "one." One wouldn't have to be June Cleaver.

RYU. Huh.

Are you hungry? I'm starving.

KATHA. Again?

RYU. How about this. How about we order in, we get a bottle of wine, get out some actual *plates*. And then maybe later we can… *(He means have sex.)*

KATHA. I told you, it's icky when you plan it.

RYU. It's been two months.

KATHA. Six weeks.

RYU. Got it. No sex.

KATHA. No *planning*.

RYU. Oh, fine, so I'll just come and take you in the night sometime, is that what you'd prefer?

(Pause. A feeling like maybe it is. RYU takes out his cell.)

Sushi or Middle Eastern?

KATHA. I don't know. Was there sushi in the '50s?

RYU. Doubtful.

KATHA. They probably didn't even have take-out. It'd be, "Honey, fix me my dinner."

RYU. Now it's starting to sound good.

KATHA. *(a deterrent)* Remember I'd be the one doing the cooking.

RYU. You have your moments. You make a good grilled cheese.

(She makes an ironic "I'm the champion of the world" gesture.)

So sushi? Say yes, 'cause I'm dialing.

KATHA. *(almost to herself)* I used to make a good red sauce.

RYU. Dragon Roll?

KATHA. I wonder if we could.

RYU. What.

KATHA. Do it, I wonder if we could live there.

RYU. You're being serious?

(He looks at her. She looks at him. He closes the phone.)

KATHA. They do trial periods. Just six months, to see.

RYU. Six months?

KATHA. Although he said most people don't feel settled for about a year.

RYU. You're not in your right mind. You're just reaching for anything that's different.

KATHA. Dean said you might have that reaction.

RYU. Dean said – . *(He contains his sudden anger.)*
I want to make sure I understand. A man you just met in the *park* is part of this cult, the Society of Dynamic – what was it?

KATHA. "Dynamic Obsolescence." The SDO for short.

RYU. And all the members of this cult –

KATHA. Why don't we find another word besides "cult" –

RYU. And all the members of this non-cult devote themselves to recreating a rigorously detailed 1950s America.

KATHA. 1955. It's always 1955.

RYU. And you are really entertaining the idea that we would leave our jobs –

KATHA. Done –

RYU. Leave our jobs and move to this gated community that just cropped up right in the middle of a landlocked Midwestern state, where we don't know anyone and we have no contact with the outside world, and we, what, we live off the land and drink ice cream sodas and pretend there's no internet?

(Short pause)

KATHA. It sounds better when you say it out loud, doesn't it.

10.

*(**ELLEN** speaks directly to us. She smokes, wonderfully. This time **DEAN** is standing farther off, just out of the light.)*

ELLEN. Here are some things you've never heard of:

Hummus.

Baba Ganoush.

Falafel.

Focaccia

Ciabatta

Whole grain bread.

(She raises her eyebrows significantly: "Yes, not even whole-grain bread.")

Portobello mushrooms

Shiitake mushrooms

Chipotle peppers

Chipotle anything.

Jamaican Jerk.

Miso.

Sushi.

That one is hard for me.

But I do without.

You'll do without too.

Gruyere

Manchego

Parmiggiano Reggiano – the parmesan in a can is all right.

No Kalamata olives

No pine nuts

No pesto

No *Lattes.*

That's hard for a lot of people.

ELLEN. *(cont.)* What you get
>   Is salt.
>   You get pepper.
>   Mayonnaise. Mustard.
>   You get dried oregano.
>   Bay leaves.
>   Paprika, if you want a little kick.
>   Sanka.
>   It's a relief, the limitations. You'll find that it's a relief.

>   It may be hard to maintain a vegetarian lifestyle. Some people have tried. You're always welcome to try, if it coincides with the rest of your Dossier. For instance, it might coincide with the Dossier of a beatnik English professor – but if you're taking on the identity of an oil man or an ad executive, it would be pretty disruptive not to have steak and a martini for lunch.

>   Disrupting means you're not period-appropriate.

>   One question we get a lot is health concerns.
>   "Do I *have* to smoke?"
>   "Do I *have* to drink?"
>   "Do I *have* to eat hot fudge sundaes."

>   Of course, we can't ask for more commitment than you're willing to give. But we think you will get much more out of the experience with total commitment, total authenticity.

>   What's a little hypertension if you're happy.

11.

(Split scene: **ELLEN** *is rummaging through* **KATHA***'s closet;* **RYU** *is elsewhere with* **DEAN***.)*

ELLEN. Just once a year. During recruiting season.

KATHA. It must be hard, coming back.

ELLEN. Not at all.

KATHA. You don't get, I don't know, *tempted?* "Ooh, HBO." "Ooh, internet."

ELLEN. Mostly I'm just reminded how hard it was. When I see all the really desperate cases.

(This hangs in the air.)

KATHA. Well. What's the prognosis?

ELLEN. You can keep the ones with cotton, wool, or silk. But throw out the poly-blends.

KATHA. Throw out?

ELLEN. Or storage. But most people decide to stay after the trial period. It doesn't really matter, as long as you keep them out of the SDO. The same goes for Lycra, ultrasuede – most of it wasn't in homes until the '70s. No digital timepieces, of course. And absolutely no Velcro *anything.*

KATHA. Isn't that always the rule?

ELLEN. Oh, you're a funny one.

KATHA. I don't know…

ELLEN. *(cheerful in a slightly metallic way)* No, it's good to know what your skills are.

*(***ELLEN** *disappears into the deep recesses of the closet. A pair of sneakers comes flying on.)*

(off) Oh dear. Most of these will have to go.

KATHA. I thought this was just a consultation?

(Over to **DEAN** *and* **RYU***.* **DEAN** *makes notes on a clipboard.)*

DEAN. Of course there are certain things about your situation that will limit your Dossier.

RYU. My situation.

DEAN. Yours and Katha's.

RYU. Katha's and mine.

DEAN. Oh dear, I'm not making myself clear. When we have a mixed-race couple, that tends to suggest certain details about their Dossier. *(He glances down at his clipboard.)* You'd be living in the North, I imagine?

RYU. North of what?

DEAN. The Mason-Dixon.

(Pause)

RYU. There's a Mason-Dixon line in the gated community?

DEAN. We have everything in microcosm, yes. So there are areas with the spirit of the South and areas that have more the feeling of the North. The Midwest. The West is still under construction, so that won't be an option for another year or two.

RYU. Well, then – I guess we would probably live in the North, yes.

DEAN. *(looking at the clipboard)* How do you feel about boxes?

RYU. Boxes?

(Back to **ELLEN** *and* **KATHA**. **ELLEN** *is holding up a frock on a hanger.)*

ELLEN. This one will work nicely.

KATHA. That was my mother's.

ELLEN. And this one.

(Pause)

KATHA. That's it?

ELLEN. And the solid-color sweaters. I'm afraid you have a very synthetic closet.

KATHA. What am I supposed to wear?

ELLEN. I sew all my own clothes now. I'll teach you. It's simple if you use patterns, and fun. You'll want to change your hair, of course. And you'll probably want to try out the support undergarments before you get to the SDO. You can find a lot of them online. There's a whole different architecture to the undergarments. It really helps with period posture and bearing.

KATHA. Is it the same for everyone?

I mean, I'm sure the beatnik chicks aren't wearing girdles, right?

ELLEN. Beatnik chicks.

KATHA. I just don't know if the whole housewife thing is the way I want to go.

(Pause)

ELLEN. Sure, smoking reefer and reading Ginsberg is fun for a day.

But you seem like you'd want something more complicated. *(enticing)* Some repression, some rich subtext. Someone you can really grow into.

KATHA. Repression…

ELLEN. In the '50s, people keep things to themselves. They hold their heads high. People have a lot of secrets.

(Beat)

I know, you think a housewife is just someone in a pretty dress. But a housewife makes things *work*. If there's a silence, she fills it. If there's a wound, she dresses it.

You're a tall girl, Kathy –

KATHA. Oh, it's "Katha."

ELLEN. *(cheerful)* I know what I said.

You're a tall girl. If you didn't slouch so much *(She corrects **KATHA**'s posture.)*, you could really command a room.

KATHA. And that's…allowed, in 1955?

*(**ELLEN** checks to make sure they're alone.)*

ELLEN. It's different for girls. It's a different kind of power. It's not about shaking a big stick. We aren't trying to be men. What we do is more indirect. But in the end, we get what we want.

(They share a smile. Back to **RYU** *and* **DEAN**.*)*

DEAN. The nice thing is you can do a trial period. So if it turns out it isn't a fit, you're free to leave at any time.

RYU. Why does that always have an ominous ring to it?

DEAN. Maybe because you're a distrustful person.

RYU. Excuse me?

DEAN. *(warm, frank)* How can you be any other way in a big city? Identity fraud, online profiles... All of your information is just – out there. That's one of the things people love about the SDO. There's less information. A kind of privacy long since extinct. A more innocent world to raise the kids in.

You do want children, don't you?

(Beat)

RYU. We tried, once. And Katha...lost it at twenty weeks, so

DEAN. I'm sorry

RYU. So I want to try again. But Katha – isn't so sure.

DEAN. Not yet.

(Pause. They lock eyes.)

For many women, that becomes very important after moving to the SDO.

*(***RYU*** *stands up.)*

RYU. I should see how Katha's doing.

DEAN. Listen, Ryu. Just listen for a second. I want to ask you something. Have you ever gone hiking for the day in the clean air and come back feeling refreshed?

RYU. Sure.

DEAN. You stand up straighter, right? You think more clearly. Everything's better when you come back, at least until that feeling wears off. So then: Why do you ever come back?

(**KATHA** *comes in wearing one of the dresses that passed muster. Her hair is up in a kerchief* **ELLEN** *gave her. She does a little twirl.*)

KATHA. *(to* **RYU***)* Well? What do you think?

ELLEN. I love it.

RYU. *(to* **KATHA***)* Can we talk alone please?

DEAN. Absolutely, what a great idea. Take your time.

(**DEAN** *and* **ELLEN** *stand a ways off, but don't exit. They watch* **RYU** *and* **KATHA** *during the following.*)

KATHA. I know what you're going to say.

RYU. What am I going to say.

KATHA. That this is all crazy,

That it'll never work,

That they're a couple of irony-free androids and what if everyone there is like them.

RYU. *(impressed and a little bewildered)* That *is* what I was going to say.

(*They glance at* **DEAN** *and* **ELLEN**. **ELLEN** *waves.*)

KATHA. They're not going to be our best friends.

They're not going to be coming over for Tupperware parties every day.

It's still going to be You and Me, without all the things that make it impossible for us to be You and Me here.

DEAN. How are you folks doing over there?

KATHA. Fine, just another minute!

RYU. *(sotto voce)* He called us a Mixed-Race Couple.

KATHA. We *are* a mixed-race couple.

RYU. But he said it with capital letters.

(*She gives him a "You're being paranoid" look.*)

You know how much I'd be making there? Four figures.

KATHA. Money goes farther there. It's adjusted for inflation. Deflation.

RYU. I went to medical school, Katha.

KATHA. You're the one who's always talking about the hours. The emptiness. The injecting goo into trophy wives who think you're their best friend. Give it six months. Think of it like a vacation. A vacation from your life. And if you miss all that, I'm sure they'll be dying to have you back.

(Beat)

Do you love your job?

RYU. No.

KATHA. Do you love your life?

RYU. No.

KATHA. Do you love me?

RYU. Yes.

12.

DEAN. The more people who come to the community, the more accuracy we're capable of. So it's not just good because Hey, the more the merrier – it's good because everyone who joins us contributes to the authenticity.

Our city planners are a good example. You see, fifty years ago, the roads were narrower and the sidewalks were wider. Did you know that? And our city planners make sure that is accurately represented. A lot of times they'll work together with the landscape architects. So we have city parks that are spotless for the nice neighborhoods. Fountains and everything, really nice. And we have parks with graffiti for the neighborhoods that maybe aren't as nice. The kind where homosexuals and communists might meet at night. There might be candy wrappers on the grass. The trees might have the names of lovers carved in them. The graffiti was a lot tamer back then, of course. We have a pamphlet for that.

Some of the technology has been hard to track down. Typewriter ribbon, mimeographs. Our engineers had to learn how to replicate them. Now they can do it so it's just like new. I mean just like old.

(ELLEN laughs wholesomely.)

This is all to say, you might want to think about how *you* can contribute. And if you can't think of something, you might consider joining your local Authenticity Committee. Ellen can tell you about that, she's the Vice President.

ELLEN. Six years running.

DEAN. My wife, a woman of influence.

13.

(Back at the office. **OMAR** *sits at* **KATHA***'s desk now.* **KATHA** *stands behind him, training him. They both look at the computer screen.)*

KATHA. I usually dump the Unsoliciteds in this folder.

OMAR. "Siberia." Cute.

KATHA. That way they aren't haunting me before I have time to deal with them.

Usually I give myself an hour on Friday morning and just burn through them. There's this one guy, Mr. Firestone? He must be in his eighties at least. He sends us all his war stories, and I mean war stories like *war.* Korea. Really, um, representational. And he always calls, asking for the hard copy back. We don't do that. He knows we don't do that. He's just looking for a way to get me on the phone – I mean you.

OMAR. Um, Katha, I wanted to thank you...

KATHA. Thank me?

OMAR. I don't want this to be weird, but you really made my career, by leaving I mean.

KATHA. Well, you can have it.

OMAR. I know I can.

KATHA. No, I mean, I don't want anything to do with it.

OMAR. You really burned out.

KATHA. I don't know if that's the word I'd–.

Fine, I "burned out."

OMAR. Do you have any advice for me?

KATHA. Advice...

OMAR. I mean, to not burn out like you?

KATHA. Um. Take breaks. Try to punch out at five. I don't know.

With you I sense a... *(as though she's saying "ruthlessness")* stability I didn't have, so.

*(***OMAR** *smiles at this.)*

OMAR. *(suddenly confidential)* Is it true you're joining a cult?

(Short pause)

That's what they're saying.

KATHA. Who.

OMAR. Everyone.

KATHA. If it's easier for you to believe, then yes, it's a cult.

OMAR. What do you mean easier to believe?

KATHA. If it means you don't have to wonder which of us is crazy: Me, for leaving? Or you, for working a 60-hour week just so you can pay for an apartment the size of a matchbox, while you spend the rest of what you make buying drinks to numb yourself while you complain to your husband which makes him hate you and makes you hate yourself even more because you're supposed to be this woman, this powerful woman because that's what you're supposed to BE, except for you don't feel powerful, you feel like someone who doesn't SLEEP or DREAM or do anything but just get THROUGH it.

OMAR. Wow.

KATHA. I'm sorry, that was – not really about you, was it. Good luck. With everything, Omar. Really.

OMAR. What is this place you're going, anyway?

(Short pause)

KATHA. You know how you'll go hiking for the day in the clean air and come back feeling refreshed? You feel better, you think clearer. So then…why do you ever come back?

OMAR. I don't really go hiking, so.

(Short pause. The phone beeps. **JENNA***'s voice comes through the speaker.)*

JENNA. Fancy salads?

OMAR. *(pressing a button on the phone, leaning towards it)* Totally.

JENNA. Is she still there?

(He looks at **KATHA***, sheepish.)*

OMAR. Yeah, we're just finishing up in here.

(The phone beeps a farewell sound.)

Sorry. You were saying?

KATHA. No. That was all.

14.

(ELLEN speaks out. DEAN stands farther off.)

ELLEN. We take our job very seriously on the Authenticity Committee. It's not just clothes and mimeograph machines – it's about everyone's *emotional* experience. And the question we have to answer again and again is how far do you take it.

We have people from all walks of life in the SDO. And the question sometimes is how do we respond authentically to these people. For instance, we have a Japanese-American fellow moving in right now. And it's interesting, what the research tells us, what we have by 1955 is already a kind of *counter*-prejudice... People have started to feel a little uncomfortable that American citizens were interned, during the war? So prejudice might not look like "Get out of my neighborhood." It might look more like "Here, I baked you some cookies, neighbor." Of course, it isn't always cookies. *(Beat)* It can be complicated to navigate, but authenticity is very important to us.

(DEAN comes forward to join her. His arm around her shoulder, supportively.)

DEAN. The SDO is...*built* on the idea of giving up one kind of freedom for another kind of freedom. Ellen and I had to give things up. *(Beat)*

But there's something about facing obstacles – it has a way of binding families together, husbands and wives. You will not believe the rewards that come from authenticity.

15.

(KATHA is holding flashcards, testing RYU.)

RYU. Eisenhower.

KATHA. Easy. Vice president?

RYU. Nixon.

KATHA. First lady.

RYU. Mamie.

KATHA. Soviet president.

RYU. Khrushchev. These are too easy.

(She flips past a few cards.)

KATHA. Best-selling car.

RYU. Chevy?

KATHA. Buick.

When was the Evacuation Claims Act?

RYU. 1948.

KATHA. *What* was the Evacuation Claims Act?

RYU. Truman agreed to compensate Japanese-Americans for their forced evacuation during the war.

KATHA. And?

RYU. And?

KATHA. How did it turn out?

RYU. Not…well.

KATHA. *(reading)* "Thirty-eight million dollars were set aside for the more than one-hundred thousand Japanese-Americans who had been moved to internment camps. But this turned out not to be nearly enough compensation to replace the decimated farms and blacklisted businesses, not to mention the emotional cost of internment." This is good stuff, this will really help you create your character.

RYU. My character.

KATHA. Well, not your "character," per se, but remember they said it's good to add details, period details, to feel emotionally – . Like maybe you have a little sister – Reiko, or Keiko…

(RYU's eyes wide at this.)

…and you had to watch her grow up in the camps. Maybe you have a lot of pent-up anger. Righteous pent-up anger.

RYU. You sound almost excited.

KATHA. I don't know, it might be a way to feel more connected.

RYU. Connected.

(Short pause)

KATHA. I just / mean

RYU. *Connected.*

KATHA. how you never talk much about your heritage, it's just never been a big thing for / you so

RYU. Oh what, because I'm not, what, doing *ikebana*? You think I'm self-hating or something? "Heritage." I'm from California, Katha, / Long Beach, California –

KATHA. Fine. Fine. Forget it.

(in the clear:)

You win. Katha is un-P.C. Bad Katha.

(Pause)

RYU. Kath. What will it be like when it's just the two of us?

KATHA. You mean –

RYU. When we're alone. Will we be us, or '50s-us?

KATHA. I think the idea is, there's no difference, if we do it right.

RYU. But will they know, if we slip?

KATHA. Like will they have our house bugged?

RYU. It's a serious question.

KATHA. In fifth grade, my favorite teacher was Mrs. Hatzlett. She taught music. I loved her class. But one time, just to show my friends I was cool, I called her Mrs. Fatslett. And soon the whole school was calling her Mrs. Fatslett.

RYU. I know this is going somewhere.

KATHA. What I'm saying is, I don't think anyone remembered that I was the one who said it first, and I don't think Mrs. Hatzlett could have *known* it was me, but – she knew. She could tell something was different because of the way I was, around her. So what I'm saying is, I think they'll know like *that*. If we've been breaking the rules.

(Short pause)

RYU. But what about, for instance, in bed.

KATHA. Oh.

RYU. Do we have to be period…

KATHA. *Oh*

RYU. …appropriate? I mean, do we have to not do things we might normally do?

KATHA. Like?

RYU. Like most of what we do!

I was reading, oral sex was illegal in 36 states.

KATHA. That doesn't mean people didn't do it.

RYU. *(conspiratorial)* True.

KATHA. As long as we can make sure it's accompanied afterward by period-accurate feelings of shame and confusion…

RYU. So it's only bad if we feel good about it?

KATHA. Yes. I think that's right.

RYU. But we're doing this to be happy in the first place…

KATHA. Right.

RYU. I'm so confused.

KATHA. I love you.

RYU. I love you too.

Let's have shame-free oral sex, while we can.

KATHA. What if we had a Safe Word.

RYU. A Safe Word. Like S&M?

KATHA. Like, absolute emergency, one of us needs to acknowledge the 21st century – absolutely *has* to talk about sushi or hybrid cars –

RYU. Or oral sex.

KATHA. But only for emergencies.

It would have to be a word no one would ever say back then.

(Pause)

RYU. "Facebook."

KATHA. Wasn't that a word?

It just meant something else.

RYU. "Twitter."

KATHA. Also a word.

RYU. This is hard.

(Pause)

KATHA. "IPad."

RYU. "X-Box."

(She makes a face.)

"Kim Kardashian."

KATHA. Something with some dignity.

(Short pause)

RYU. "Hybrid car."

KATHA. Too clunky.

(Short pause)

"Portobello."

RYU. Too whimsical.

KATHA. "Latte."

RYU. Too lame.

KATHA. "Hillary Rodham Clinton."

  (Pause)

RYU. "Hillary Rodham Clinton."

KATHA. It has *heft*, right?

RYU. You wouldn't say that by accident.

KATHA. It's modern, it's shrill – I already kind of miss it.

RYU. You sure you want to do this.

KATHA. Yes.

  Are you sure?

RYU. *("you promise?")* Six months.

  (She nods.)

  Goodbye Hillary.

KATHA. Goodbye Hillary.

RYU. Hello Ike.

  (Short pause)

KATHA. "I like Ike."

  "I like Ike!"

  (He joins in. It grows into a joyful, impulsive dance.)

BOTH.

  I like Ike!

  I like Ike!

  I like Ike!

  I like Ike!

  (Blackout.)

16.

(DEAN speaks out. ELLEN looks on from a distance.)

DEAN. A lot of people ask me, Dean, isn't it hard pretending all the time?

And what I tell them is I tell them about a TV show called "The Adventures of Ozzie and Harriet." Most of you have probably heard about it, even if you haven't seen it.

Nowadays you have TV shows about people who solve crimes using ESP, and people who solve crimes with math, and people who solve crimes with talking cars.

But back then people just wanted to see a family, like their own family but a bit nicer, like their own family but a bit more attractive.

(Lights rise on a modest but attractive 1950s living room.)

And what was so special about this TV family the Nelsons is that they weren't actors, not really. They were themselves. They used their own names. Ozzie, Harriet, David, and Ricky. They got up every morning and drove to the studio a few minutes away, and they ate their breakfast in a dining room modeled after their own dining room, but a little bit cleaner.

(KATHA enters, wearing a housedress and a short new period haircut. She goes by KATHY now. She pulls the curtains open and looks out into the sunny morning.)

And they acted out their own problems and obstacles, only those problems were a little smaller, a little simpler, so you could be sure to solve them in a single episode. And a curious thing: The longer they pretended, the less they could tell what was pretend and what was real.

(The doorbell rings.)

KATHY. Who could that be?

DEAN. So it's kind of funny to me when people get so suspicious of pretending. I mean, don't you think people pretend every day, without knowing it?

We all imagine the life we'd like to have, and it takes a little pretend to get it.

(**KATHY** *opens the door.*)

(*There are two beautiful bottles of fresh milk resting on the welcome mat.*)

End of Part One

PART TWO

1.

(Sounds of a factory – a nice, clean, civilized factory. **ROGER** *is showing* **RYU** *around. They both wear work uniforms.* **ROGER** *is played by the same actor who played* **OMAR**. *Much more stoic now.)*

ROGER. [We call that the Crow's Nest. Managers can see pretty much everything from up there. Who's working and who ain't, if you catch my drift.]* This floor is all Boxers. Lots of fellas start out here. The Packers are one floor down, and below that you've got Secretarial.

RYU. Specialized.

ROGER. There you go.

(ROGER picks up an un-made cardboard box. While he's talking, he assembles it with effortless quickness and grace. Almost involuntary.)

First thing is to make sure you do the narrow flaps first, before the wide flaps. Then you want to add a dot of glue to each corner. Dot, dot, dot, dot. No more than a dot or it turns into a mess. *Now* it's time for the wide flaps. Then you got your tape, make sure it's nice and wet. Then it goes snip, and down the chute.

(He pushes the completed box down a chute.)

RYU. Got it.

ROGER. Why don't you do one for me.

(RYU starts to make a box. He folds the narrow flaps first.)

Good...

---

* Optional cut for production.

RYU. So. Is this…fulfilling?

ROGER. What?

RYU. Here at the factory – is it gratifying?

ROGER. I'm not sure I know what you mean. The work isn't too hard. You get thirty minutes for lunch. The owner is nice.

RYU. Yeah?

ROGER. He says hello when you pass him in the hall. Every June there's a picnic at his place. His wife makes potato salad and there's a three-legged race. Madge and I won last year.

RYU. *(sincere)* That sounds…good.

ROGER. You came from the big city, right?

RYU. That's right.

ROGER. What'd you do back there?

RYU. *(not looking at* ROGER*)* Taxi driver.

ROGER. Must meet some crazies doing that.

RYU. It was all right.

ROGER. You folks find a place to stay?

RYU. Yeah, over on Maple and Vine?

ROGER. Over by the high school, right?

RYU. It's two blocks away. Little yellow ranch house.

ROGER. Oh yeah, that used to be the Gibson place.

RYU. Oh. Where'd they go?

(The slightest pause)

ROGER. Moved somewhere bigger, I imagine. Very ambitious guy, Donner Gibson. Had a mulatto wife, but she was so light you might not even know it. Probably fooled some people. Gibson was at the steel mill, last I heard. They like to move people up over there. Here too. You won't be a Boxer for long if you've got the drive. And nobody doubts you little guys have the drive, right? Not anymore.

(Beat)

I mean after the war.

RYU. Oh, right.

ROGER. *Kamikaze.* Those little guys had drive, you gotta hand it to them.

RYU. *(playing along, hoping this will end)* Oh, yeah, you better watch out.

ROGER. There you go. So, I'm gonna leave you to it. If it takes you more than 30 seconds a box, you're probably too slow. And you'll keep getting faster. Just give me a holler if you need anything.

RYU. Okay, thanks.

    *(***RYU*** finishes the box. He lifts it up. A feeling of small satisfaction.)*

2.

(**KATHY** *has been setting out hors d'oeuvres. She wears a cocktail dress. Something smooth is playing on the hi-fi.*)

(**RYU** *comes in, wiping sweat off his brow.*)

RYU. Hi.

KATHY. How was your first day?

RYU. Well it's not exactly rocket science, but – I started out okay and I got better. Thirty seconds a box. It's more physical than you'd think.

KATHY. I can see that.

RYU. You fall behind and forget about it.

KATHY. Better wash up. The Messners will be here any minute.

RYU. Shit, I forgot.

KATHY. You'll be fine, it's only cocktails. Just put on a clean shirt. And a spritz of that cologne I got you.

(*The doorbell rings.*)

Oh dear, that's them. Hurry – oh wait, do these look okay?

RYU. (*smirking*) You cooked?

KATHY. I cook every night, remember?

(*She winks at him.*)

RYU. Oh, yeah.

KATHY. Try one.

RYU. What are they?

(*He pops one in his mouth.*)

KATHY. Pigs in a blanket.

RYU. (*with a mouthful*) Sauce is good.

KATHY (*proud*) It's ketchup and mayo.

(*Ding dong. The doorbell again.* **KATHY** *goes to the door,* **RYU** *heads off.*)

Coming!

(*She opens the door.* **DEAN** *and* **ELLEN** *are standing* *there.* **ELLEN** *holds a wrapped present.)*

DEAN. Hello, hello!

KATHY. Ellen, Dean. Won't you come in? Oh –

ELLEN. *(handing her the gift)* It's just a little something for the house.

KATHY. You shouldn't have.

*(***ELLEN** *looks around. She might be inspecting things for authenticity, but disguises it as the curiosity of a house-guest.)*

ELLEN. Looks like you're all moved in…

KATHY. We're nearly there, yes. *(comically miming a pain in her back)* Oof.

DEAN. "Oof?"

KATHY. All those boxes. But the neighbors have been wonderful. Heavy lifting. Bringing *pies.*

DEAN. Well what d'you expect? They're your neighbors.

KATHY. We just never had such – visible neighbors! *(almost to herself)* Audible maybe.

ELLEN. *(still inspecting)* It's a charming house. I've always thought it was charming from the street but this is even nicer.

*(***DEAN** *hands* **KATHY** *his hat and* **ELLEN'***s coat.)*

KATHY. Oh, sorry.

Please, won't you sit down.

What can I get you all to drink?

ELLEN. Dubonnet, please.

DEAN. Yes, I'll have a Dubonnet too. With ice.

ELLEN. *(nodding)* Ice.

KATHY. Two Dubonnets.

(Just as **KATHY** *heads off to make the drinks, something strikes the outside of the window.)*

ELLEN. What was that?

DEAN. I think it was…something hitting the outside of the house.

(Something hits the window again. It's a pebble.)

ELLEN. Oh how strange.

DEAN. I better go see what it is.

KATHY. *(reentering with drinks)* Did that come from outside?

DEAN. Probably just some neighborhood urchins.

ELLEN. Be careful, Darling.

DEAN. Don't be silly.

> *(**DEAN** goes out the door.)*

ELLEN. Oh how strange.

> *(Maybe it doesn't sound like **ELLEN** thinks it's all that strange.)*
>
> *(Light shifts to outside the house. **ROGER** is there, in the shadows, pebble in hand.)*

DEAN. How dare you.

ROGER. How dare I?

DEAN. Ellen is in there, we're with friends – this is very embarrassing.

ROGER. You made your excuses.

DEAN. How did you know I'd be here?

ROGER. You always check in with the newbies the first week. And he said Maple and Vine.

DEAN. You did your homework.

ROGER. You wanted to see me too.

DEAN. What are you talking about.

ROGER. That's why you placed him on my floor.

DEAN. They all start out in Boxing, especially the Negros and Orientals.

ROGER. Or else in Packing – or the steel mill, or anywhere! But no, he's right there with me, on my watch. Like some kind of message.

DEAN. I told you to leave me alone, remember?

ROGER. Guess I forgot.

> *(He pulls **DEAN** into a kiss. They kiss forcefully, angrily. **ROGER** starts to touch **DEAN**.)*

ROGER. Say it.

DEAN. Say what.

ROGER. You know what. Say it.

DEAN. *(barely audible)* I want you to fuck me.

ROGER. What was that?

DEAN. I want you to fuck me.

ROGER. What are we going to do about that?

(*Short pause*)

DEAN. The park at midnight.
    Ellen sleeps like a log.

ROGER. I remember.

(*Beat*)

God I miss fucking you.

DEAN. I'm not like you.
    I don't need this.

ROGER. Could have fooled me.

DEAN. Get the hell out of here.

(*Back inside the house.* **KATHY** *has just opened the present.*)

ELLEN. It's a tea cozy.

KATHY. Oh, how wonderful. We don't have one!

ELLEN. It's supposed to be a frog.

KATHY. I think I see it.

ELLEN. It's, what's the word, abstract.

(**RYU** *enters.*)

RYU. Hello Ellen.

(**ELLEN** *bows slightly.*)

ELLEN. Hello.

KATHY. Look what Ellen brought us.

ELLEN. I have a friend who knits them, she's very talented.
    You'll meet her soon.

(**DEAN** *reenters.* **RYU** *shakes his hand.*)

RYU. Mr. Messner.

DEAN. Please, Ryu. Call me Dean.

ELLEN. Is everything all right?

DEAN. Of course. Fellow lost his way, he was looking for Elm. So I told him he had his trees mixed up.

(**DEAN** *laughs at his own joke.*)

ELLEN. You should have invited him in.

DEAN. Oh, no. He didn't look like a very sociable fellow, I'm afraid. Not one of ours.

KATHY. I should say not, throwing rocks at people's windows. Hasn't he heard of a knocker?

(*We hear a buzzer from off stage.*)

Oh, those are my crab puffs.

(*She goes. A short but heavy silence.*)

ELLEN. (*to* **DEAN**) They loved the cozy.

RYU. We did, we loved it.

KATHY. (*from off*) We did!

ELLEN. Tell me, Ryu – Did everyone make you feel at home at the factory?

RYU. Very much. The Floor Manager was nice. Fellow named Roger.

ELLEN. (*This might be directed toward* **DEAN**, *lightly.*) How nice.

RYU. He seemed sort of…preoccupied with my heritage?

ELLEN. Some people are still adjusting. To think, just a few years ago we were putting you people behind fences, and now you're working right there alongside us. Isn't it grand. *America.*

(**KATHY** *returns with the crab puffs just in time to hear this. She and* **RYU** *share a wide-eyed look from across the room.*)

KATHY. I'm a little nervous how these turned out, this is a brand-new recipe for me.

DEAN. It smells delicious.

KATHY. I know crab is a trifle *exotic,* but you put cream cheese in anything and it's bound to turn out well.

DEAN. Mmm.

ELLEN. Well, aren't these nice and simple.

(ELLEN deposits the rest of hers in a napkin.)

RYU. These are *really good,* Honey.

(Short pause. ELLEN sees that DEAN is unusually quiet, she'll have to keep the conversation going.)

ELLEN. You should come with me to the Authenticity Committee sometime, Kathy.

KATHY. *(non-committal)* That would be nice.

ELLEN. Monday, Wednesday and Friday in the school gymnasium. We'd love to have you.

(DEAN and RYU chew solemnly.)

(ELLEN discreetly corrects KATHY's posture.)

Remember...

(There is a kind of cut – Lights down and up again quickly. Everyone is playing charades now. They're all a bit tipsy. ELLEN takes the game very seriously, her true colors showing. It's KATHY's turn, she mimes a movie camera.)

Movie!

Four words.

Fourth word.

Four syllables.

(KATHY acts bored. She mimes looking at a watch. She taps her foot.)

RYU. Um.

"Waiting."

"Boredom?"

(KATHY acts even more emphatically bored.)

"Impatient."

ELLEN. *(chastening)* Four. Syllables.

(**KATHY** *makes a gesture for clearing the first attempt away, starting over.*)

(*She starts to wrap her arms around herself, rather embarrassed, as if to suggest a couple making out.*)

DEAN. "From Here To Eternity!"

KATHY. YES!

(**ELLEN** *and* **RYU** *look at* **DEAN**, *amazed.*)

DEAN. I love that movie.

(*Another cut, lights abruptly down and up. The two couples are now slow dancing to a waltz on the hi-fi.* **RYU** *is struggling. Still, it's fun.*)

It helps to count at first.

DEAN & ELLEN. One-two-three, one-two-three.

RYU. One-two-three, one-two-three.

DEAN. With the emphasis on the *one*-two-three.

RYU. *One*-two-three, *one*-two-three.

KATHY. That's it.

DEAN. *(speaking in waltz rhythm)* And then, when you're comfortable with that...

(*He gives* **ELLEN** *a twirl.*)

ELLEN. Ta da.

(*Another cut, lights down and up. Everyone in different positions, a bit drunker now.* **RYU** *is pouring himself another drink.* **ELLEN** *is telling one of her favorite stories.*)

So I said to the girl seated next to me, I said Lorna there's nothing I hate more than a *soggy cake*. And what does the hostess come in with, right that very moment?

KATHY. A soggy cake!

DEAN. Right!

ELLEN. *(mimicking the hostess entering proudly)* "*Baba au Rhum.*" This enormous rum-soaked thing. I was so embarrassed.

DEAN. So she ate every bite on her plate.

KATHY. Oh that's so funny. Isn't that funny, Ryu?

RYU. Does anyone need a refresher?

DEAN. You know what I'd love? A vodka rocks.

RYU. Grey Goose okay?

DEAN. Grey Goose, what's that?

RYU. Vodka, my friend.

ELLEN. No, he means: *What's that.*

RYU. Oh you mean –

KATHY. *(suddenly sober)* We're so sorry.

DEAN. That's all right, it happens to everyone.

KATHY. I'll pour it out.

DEAN. Gin will be fine, Ryu.

ELLEN. Smirnoff. That's a kind of Vodka we like.
They've been making it such a long time.

(Another cut. DEAN and ELLEN are gone now. KATHY and RYU are splayed on the couch.)

KATHY. Well that wasn't so bad, was it?

RYU. I don't know about Ellen.

KATHY. I think she's just…shy.

(They lock eyes for a moment. Then, overlapping:)

KATHY & RYU. "Four Syllables!"

KATHY. Oh dear. Well, I think we're off the hook for a
while. I better get to work on this.

RYU. Let me help you.

KATHY. Nonsense. That's my job.

*(She starts to clear the plates. RYU lying on his back on
the couch.)*

RYU. *(content)* I'm beat.

KATHY. You had a long day.

(She continues to clear. RYU sits up suddenly.)

RYU. Kath.

KATHY. Mm?

RYU. "Hillary Rodham Clinton."

(Short pause)

KATHY. *(sotto voce)* Already?

RYU. I'm sorry.

KATHY. What is it?

RYU. I think I saw something tonight.

KATHY. You saw something?

RYU. It was Dean.
     Outside.

3.

(Split scene. At the factory, **RYU** *assembles a box while* **ROGER** *times him.)*

ROGER. Ready,

Set,

Go.

(At the same time, **KATHY** *stands in the kitchen, squinting at an open cookbook.)*

KATHY. "Celery is often underrated, yet it can be the secret star of any dish. First, cut the stalks lengthwise. Then cut crosswise to dice. Try to make the dice as small and uniform as possible, both because it is aesthetically more pleasing and because the small pieces will cook more uniformly."

*(***KATHY** *starts to dice an onion, just as* **RYU** *finishes the box.)*

ROGER. Twenty-two seconds.

You sure you haven't made boxes before?

RYU. No. But I used to work with my hands.

ROGER. Thought you said you were a taxi driver.

(Short pause)

RYU. Oh, I mean back before.

ROGER. *(nodding solemnly)* Back in the old country...

RYU. I did *Ikebana.* You know what that is?

ROGER. Something with knives.

RYU. Flowers. Flower arranging. It's not so different really – the planes of the petals, the sort of minimalist thing.

ROGER. I gotta say, your English is – wow.

RYU. *(a touch ironic)* Thank you. I work hard.

ROGER. Make a better life for the Missus. I get it.

Hey, tell me something about her.

RYU. Well, she's um, she's pretty as a picture.

ROGER. *(playful)* Yeah, but can she cook.

RYU. She's getting there.

(Light shifts to **KATHY***, who has returned to the cookbook.)*

KATHY. "Strain liquid through a fine mesh strainer into another large stockpot." *(looking around)* Fine mesh strainer...

(And back to the factory.)

ROGER. Name's Kathy, right?

RYU. Kathy, yeah.

ROGER. She must be something else.

I mean, if you'd do all this for her.

(Short pause. How much does **ROGER** *know about them?)*

RYU. When we lived in the city, sometimes it was like I never saw her. Even when I was with her I never saw her. But here, it's like...

ROGER. You see her.

RYU. But you know how it is, you've got a wife.

(Pause. **ROGER** *just smiles.)*

RYU. Was it...her idea, to come here?

ROGER. *(with a rueful smile, not answering the question)* It's always someone's idea, right?

RYU. Women can be pretty persuasive.

(Maybe **ROGER** *gets rather close to* **RYU** *here.)*

ROGER. Some friendly advice, Ryu. *(He pronounces it "Rye-You.")* I've seen guys come here, they're used to letting their wives wear the pants. Guys who don't learn how to wear the pants, they don't fit in too well.

RYU. Did you ever...

ROGER. What.

RYU. Not fit in? *(returning to the boxes:)* I'm sorry.

ROGER. *(coded)* Sometimes, when people come here, it means making sacrifices, socially speaking.

RYU. *(coded)* And does that work out...for people?

ROGER. I'll let you know when I find out.

(**ROGER** *exits. The phone rings in* **KATHY**'s *space. The factory light fades.*)

KATHY. Hello?

—

Ellen, hello!

—

No, no. Just wrestling with *mirepoix*.

—

Oh. Well, you're kind to think of me. I just hope I have something to wear. Do you think gloves are too much?

—

To the wrist. Of course.

(**KATHY** *laughs, scandalized by something* **ELLEN** *says.*)

Opera length! In the afternoon?

RYU. *(off)* Honey?

(**RYU** *comes in.*)

KATHY. No, no, thank *you*. To tell you the truth, it was getting a little quiet around here.

—

Perfect. 2 o'clock. Bye now.

(*She hangs up.*)

That was Ellen. I'm going to the committee with her tomorrow.

RYU. She finally wore you down, huh.

KATHY. I don't know, it might be fun. How was work?

RYU. I'm down to twenty-two seconds.

KATHY. That's wonderful.

RYU. Closing in on the record.

KATHY. How are things with the boss?

RYU. Now I'm an ikebana master. In addition to banzai and karate.
He said he'd never seen a foreigner learn so fast.

(**KATHY** *shakes her head, bemused.*)

RYU. Is it bad it feels kind of good?

KATHY. What.

RYU. Low expectations.

KATHY. I'll forgive you if you forgive me.

My main accomplishment today was learning the difference between chop and dice.

RYU. And?

KATHY. Dice means I only cut off a small piece of my finger.

RYU. What did you make?

KATHY. Chicken stock. *(Beat)*

It was amazing, Ryu. It took *seven hours.*

I had to chop, I had to dice, I boiled the water.

I skimmed, I strained. Things changed shape. Chemistry.

When it was done – there was something there that wasn't there before.

RYU. So we're having chicken stock for dinner.

KATHY. I made something. With my hands. I know it sounds small.

RYU. It doesn't.

(Beat)

KATHY. I think I might be a little happy.

4.

*(***KATHY*** *is having a dream.* **JENNA** *and* **OMAR** *sit sprawled in her living room. Suburban quiet now, in place of the din of the first sleeping scene.)*

KATHY. Kathy slept through the night now. There were crickets outside her window for lulling her to sleep. Kathy had dreams every night now, but every night she dreamed about the world she'd left behind.

JENNA. Fancy salad place?

OMAR. Always.

JENNA. I can never make up my mind. So many dressings.

OMAR. I know, right?

JENNA. I think I'll get the chipotle-balsamic.

OMAR. *("it's your funeral")* Indulge.

JENNA. *(crestfallen)* I thought it was low-fat.

OMAR. Not like the ginger-miso. You get the chipotle-balsamic, you might as well be having a whole foccaccia.

JENNA. The foccaccia's lower-cal than the ciabatta, right?

OMAR. Not like the parmesan flatbread.

So. I was eye-flirting with this guy at the gym – he was, *Oh.*

JENNA. "Oh." What's "oh"?

(He raises an eyebrow.)

I mean I know what "oh" is but I want *details.*

OMAR. Let's just say he's not having the ciabatta.

*(***DEAN*** *enters.)*

DEAN. Excuse me.

OMAR. Here he is now.

DEAN. Do you know where 200 Fifth Avenue is?

OMAR. You just found it, Mister.

DEAN. Oh. Thank you.

*(***OMAR*** *and* **DEAN** *start to neck.)*

JENNA. *(faux-annoyed)* You guys, we're right here.

KATHY. You're – in the wrong place.

(**OMAR** *and* **DEAN** *still necking, deeply. Shirts are coming off.*)

JENNA. Tell me about it. Like get a room, right?

KATHY. No, I mean – Everyone's in the wrong place.

JENNA. Kind of hot though. Least somebody's getting some.

(**OMAR** *starts to pull* **DEAN** *off stage.* **JENNA** *follows them.*)

You guys, where are you going?

RYU. Kathy?

OMAR. To get a room.

(**RYU** *enters.*)

KATHY. Everyone's wrong.

RYU. Kathy?

KATHY. Everyone's –

(He touches her. **KATHY** *wakes with a start in the living room.* **RYU** *is standing next to her, his hand on her shoulder. The others are gone.)*

Wrong.

RYU. Shhh, you're okay. You were sleepwalking again.

KATHY. Where are we?

RYU. Home.

KATHY. I mean – when?

RYU. 1955.

(Beat)

Come back to bed.

KATHY. I'm going to sit up a little while.

RYU. You sure?

KATHY. Just until things settle.

(Beat)

Do you ever…forget?

RYU. Sometimes, when I first wake up.
But then there's the wallpaper.

(She takes in the dark living room.)

And you in your nightie.

(He tugs at the hem of her nightie.)

KATHY. My mind is racing.

RYU. I have an idea.

KATHY. Warm milk?

(He lowers to his knees.)

RYU. Close your eyes.

KATHY *(she does)* Why?

RYU. Just relax.

(He starts to lift up her slip.)

KATHY. What are you doing?

RYU. You know what.

KATHY. Baby, I don't think / we should –

RYU. What are you afraid of? The neighbors aren't watching.

KATHY. What if they are?

RYU. Close your eyes.

(He starts to kiss her under her nightgown.)

5.

(ELLEN speaks directly out. She is seated now, address-
ing an unseen circle of people.)

ELLEN. Well ladies. I wanted to talk today about a bit of
a touchy subject. Contraception. As you know, we've
been letting people determine their own boundaries.
But it seems to me that the disruptions have become…
rather disruptive. For instance, when I go to the drug
store, I'm just a bit surprised to see a long line of ladies
getting their prescriptions filled for birth control. I'm
surprised to see Catholic families, prominent Catholic
families, with only a single child. And very recently a
girlfriend of mine was bragging that her husband was
positively cheerful in his attitude toward wearing a
condom. Cheerful!

What's to be done. Well, there's the usual letters to the
editor. But I think we should consider drafting a bill.
The birth-control pill wasn't in homes until 1960 – as
long as it remains available, women will continue to
disrupt. The ability to bear children is a power and
a privilege, and those of us who aren't too busy running a community must embrace that privilege, yes?
Without the birth-control pill, it would be much easier
to accurately portray a woman's role at the center of
the family, financially dependent on her husband and
rooted to the home.

Speaking of which, I want to officially welcome our
newest homemaker on the committee, Kathy Nakata.

(KATHY enters, in a smart coat and gloves to the wrist.)

KATHY. Thank you. *(to the entire group)* Thank you so much
for having me.

ELLEN. Kathy and her husband have been with us a couple
of months now.
Right now it's just the two of them.

6.

*(**KATHY** is reading a hardcover copy of* Peyton Place *while something simmers on the stove.* **RYU** *comes in the door, lunchbox in hand.)*

RYU. Honey, I'm home.

KATHY. Hi.

RYU. Something smells good.

KATHY. Chicken à la King.

RYU. My favorite.

(He plants a quick kiss on her.)

KATHY. Should be just a few more minutes.

RYU. *(re: the book)* How is that, anyway?

KATHY. Well it isn't Tolstoy. But I think she has a real narrative gift. I mean, everyone on the block is reading it.

RYU. I know – even the boys at the factory are reading it.

KATHY. I bet they're flipping forward to the cheeky parts.

RYU. You think anyone's town is really that bad?

KATHY. I'm sure.

(In another part of the stage, light on **DEAN** *and* **ROGER** *lying in a park somewhere. Post coitus.)*

DEAN. Fuck.

ROGER. Yeah. You can say that again.

(Beat)

Change of pace, fucking when it's light outside. When everyone's just sitting down to supper.

(In another part of the stage, light on **ELLEN** *at the dinner table, alone. A casserole sits in front of her, growing cold. Light remains on her during the rest of the scene.)*

DEAN. You sure this is safe?

ROGER. Sure. Never seen anyone on this side of the pond.

*(**DEAN** starts to put his clothes on.)*

Same time next week?

DEAN. Too soon.

ROGER. Too soon?

DEAN. It has to get to the point where I'm so full of...

ROGER. Cum?

DEAN. *(irritated at his coarseness) Wanting.* So full of wanting
that it...overcomes the guilt.

ROGER. Yeah, you're pretty good at the whole guilt thing.
Me, I like to think, after a long week of work, I deserve
a little present.

*(**ROGER** watches as **DEAN** puts his pants on.)*

Just a little longer. Please.

DEAN. It's nearly suppertime.

ROGER. Let her wait an hour. I waited all week.

*(He pulls **DEAN** back down by his belt loops. They kiss,
more tenderly now.)*

*(Back to **KATHY** and **RYU**.)*

KATHY. I was at the committee today.

RYU. Again?

KATHY. There was a vote.
They voted to outlaw the Pill.

RYU. They can do that?

*(a slight nod from **KATHY**)*

There are other options, right?

KATHY. Or, I was thinking. Or.
We could not worry about it.

RYU. Oh Kathy, do you mean it?

KATHY. Now that we're here. *(The hint of a contract in this:)* I
can imagine having a baby...here.

(Pause)

It's four months now.

RYU. I know.

KATHY. We have to decide sooner or later.

*(Back to **ROGER** and **DEAN**, lying down.)*

ROGER. Sometimes I wish we didn't have to hide. You know? Sometimes I wonder if there's a place like that. A place where it'd be you and me sitting down to dinner in one of those houses.

DEAN. You know, Roger. I'm not sure you understand. We don't know each other.

ROGER. What?

DEAN. You and I – we don't *talk* to each other. We got what we needed from each other, so.

(He extends his hand for a handshake. It's a punch in the gut to ROGER.*)*

ROGER. I wish you wouldn't –

(sotto voce)

I mean it's just the two of us here.

DEAN. I'll see you around.

ROGER. No you won't. You never see me, not really.

DEAN. What's going on?

ROGER. I've been thinking for once.

DEAN. *(putting on his hat)* It was a mistake to stay. I've confused you.

ROGER. This is really enough for you. You don't ever think what if it was you and me in one of those houses?

DEAN. I have a house.

ROGER. Jason. I love you.

*(*DEAN *stops in his tracks.)*

DEAN. Don't – EVER – call me that.

(Back to KATHY *and* RYU.*)*

RYU. If we decide to stay…what do we tell it?

KATHY. ?

RYU. I mean would the baby know the things we know? *(sotto voce)* He could grow up thinking there isn't anywhere else.

KATHY. Maybe that's a gift.

RYU. *(hotter)* We had a choice, to come here, but he –

KATHY. Or she.

RYU. Don't you wonder what it'd be like for *our child* – growing up here?

I just don't want it to be…hard.

"Hillary Rodham Clinton."

KATHY. No. You can do this.

*(**RYU** shakes his head. **KATHY** starts to exit toward the kitchen.)*

RYU. Like Reiko.

(This stops her.)

I was almost out of high school when we went to the camp, but Reiko was only…

(He doesn't seem to remember.)

KATHY. Seven.

RYU. Seven.

KATHY *("how awful")* God.

RYU. She was all right at the camp. She made friends so fast. It was when it was over, when we moved back home – I'll never forget watching my little sister learn she was different. The way the kids looked at her at school. The Evacuation Claims Act couldn't fix that. I don't want our little girl to go through that.

KATHY. It'll be different for her. The world is changing, one step at a time.

RYU. Is it?

KATHY. But it's 1955, not 1945. / That's what I mean.

RYU. And never 1956 or '57 / or Civil *Rights* –

KATHY. We're right smack dab in the middle of things changing – and we're the ones who get to help people change their minds!

RYU. That's fine for us – but what I'm saying is maybe our *child* deserves to know there are fifty years of history / that she's –

KATHY. Will you please try not to disrupt –

RYU. We have to TALK about this!

(He has grabbed her by the arm. He releases her.)

I'm sorry.

KATHY *(not quite meeting his gaze yet)* No, that was good.

RYU. What?

KATHY. You took charge. Remember you can do that. You're the husband.

(ELLEN stands up, hearing someone at the door.)

ELLEN. Dean? Is that you?

(DEAN comes in.)

DEAN. Darling I'm so sorry. I lost track of time.

(He kisses her on the cheek.)

ELLEN. *(lightly)* That's not like you.

(He starts to take off his coat and hat.)

KATHY. It'll still be us, every day. You have to remember that. We'll keep talking about what she has to know. I'm sure there's a pamphlet –

RYU. No. We have to decide for us. The minute we stop being us...

KATHY. What?

RYU. I don't know.

(DEAN goes to the dining table.)

DEAN. You must have been cooking for hours.

ELLEN. Oh, that's all right. I'll put the casserole back in the oven. It'll warm right up.

DEAN. It looks delicious.

ELLEN. Oh, don't sit down. There's mud on your pants.

DEAN. Well look at that. It must've been that walk in the park.

(Short pause)

ELLEN. Go put on a fresh pair, and I'll toss those right in the wash.

(He starts to go.)

DEAN. Ellen?

ELLEN. Yes?

DEAN. I'm a lucky man.

7.

(At the factory. **ROGER** *and* **RYU** *with lunchboxes.)*

RYU. Bologna and cheese.

ROGER. Turkey lettuce tomato.

RYU. Wanna trade?

ROGER. No deal.

RYU. I don't blame you.

ROGER. I mean, what *is* bologna anyway?

RYU. It's Italian. *(playful)* Very continental.

> *(***ROGER*** *leans over slowly and takes a bite of* **RYU***'s sandwich, looking at him the whole time.)*

Oh, hey, what are you, um – what do you think?

ROGER. *(still looking at him, intense)* Salty.

(Short pause)

RYU. I better get back to work.

ROGER. Hey, we got ten minutes. Stick around. I was just playing.

RYU. Sure, okay.

ROGER. You're a good worker, Ryu. I like having you around.

RYU. Thanks.

ROGER. How's Kathy liking the committee?

RYU. Too much.

ROGER. Buncha hens.

RYU. Everything else is good though. More than good.

ROGER. You wearing the pants?

RYU. I'm wearing the pants.

ROGER. That makes one of us.

(Pause)

RYU. If you ever want to talk about it…

ROGER. Thanks.

RYU. Listen, Roger –
Kathy and I are thinking of starting a family.

ROGER. Congrats, Sport! It's about time.

RYU. Yeah, and I was wondering, maybe, I was wondering, if it might be time for me to have a raise.

(Short pause)

ROGER. *(with some difficulty)* I'm sorry, Sport

RYU. Oh

ROGER. You're one of the best on the floor, but standard raise is after half a year. You've barely been here, what is it?

RYU. Five months. Stuckey was only here three when he got his.

ROGER. Sorry.

*(**ROGER** starts to go.)*

RYU. Were you at my house, a few months ago?

*(**ROGER** stops.)*

ROGER. Was I at your house?

RYU. I thought I saw you, out my window.

ROGER. Why would I be at your house?

RYU. I guess it must have been someone else.
Whoever it was, it seems like a fella could get in a heap of trouble if someone saw him.

(Pause)

ROGER. Let me tell you about a heap of trouble, Ryu.
See, I know you're really a nice guy. And I know you wouldn't want to do something to mess up your prospects here. Because I've been giving you the good word. I've seen lots of people come through here and nobody does well without the good word from the floor manager. Especially the non-whites. And if you think that it can't get worse for you than making a thousand boxes a day, then you better take a look at those poor suckers laying tar on the roads or putting spikes in the

railroad tracks. Is all I'm saying. Because I think you and the wife could do really well here, despite your being a little "different" and all, just as long as you have the good word. So why don't you keep your head down and do your work and eat your fucking bologna. See you later.

(He leaves abruptly.)

8.

(**KATHY** *at the front door.*)

KATHY. *(calling off)* Good night, Judy! I haven't forgotten about your cake pan! I'll bring it to the committee tomorrow.

(**KATHY** *comes in and turns on a lamp. She sits on the arm of the sofa. She touches her stomach, her coat still on.*)

(**RYU** *comes in suddenly, startling her.*)

How was work?

RYU. Work was shit.

KATHY. Language.

RYU. You think I give a fuck? *(Beat)*

Why don't you have your apron on?

KATHY. I'm sorry, I was –

RYU. Great, that's just great – Work is shit and no dinner isn't in the oven.

KATHY. My appointment was running late.

RYU. You're always at that fucking committee.

KATHY. It wasn't the committee.

RYU. Well it sure seems like you're always there. I'm hungry.

KATHY. There are two TV dinners in the freezer. I thought we could heat them up and watch *Lucy*.

(Short pause)

RYU. What kind?

KATHY. *(hopefully)* Salisbury steak.

(Something relaxes in **RYU**.*)*

RYU. I'm sorry I was sore.

KATHY. What happened today?

RYU. I didn't get the raise

KATHY. Oh Ryu

RYU. And then Roger got angry.

KATHY. He got angry?

RYU. When he said no – I told him what I saw.

KATHY. That night.

RYU. I thought that might change his mind.

KATHY. You mean blackmail?

RYU. I don't know, I didn't think that far. I just thought maybe then he couldn't treat me like a second-class citizen. I'm faster than everyone on that floor, Roger included.

KATHY. You'll show him. Someday you'll be running that factory.

RYU. Damn right. Damn right I will.

KATHY. I'm glad you said it. Now he knows who he's dealing with.

(Pause)

(He takes her and kisses her. Suddenly very heated.)

(They separate for a moment, surprised by this new fire.)

RYU. Even when the neighbors aren't very…neighborly? It makes me feel closer to you.

(They kiss.)

KATHY. I should – I have something to tell you.

RYU. *(still kissing her)* Let me guess. Those ladies passed another bill.

KATHY. I told you, / it wasn't –

RYU. Oh right.

KATHY. I went to see Dr. Anderson.

RYU. – .

KATHY. I'm pregnant.

RYU. Oh my god.

KATHY. You're not upset, are you?

RYU. Upset? Are you kidding?

I'm thrilled!

(He picks her up and whirls her around.)

I'm fucking ecstatic!

KATHY. *(amused)* Language!

RYU. Why would I be upset?

KATHY. I just thought, if you still weren't sure, about staying...

RYU. Oh

KATHY. *(not endorsing this)* ...then I imagine there are alternatives.

RYU. Alternatives.

(Beat)

KATHY. "Hillary Rodham" –

RYU. No. We're going to have a baby, and we're going to love it.

(He takes her hand.)

What other choice is there?

KATHY. The ladies at the committee will be so excited. They were really rooting for us. I think they really like me there. They were saying I could be a Vice President someday.

RYU. My wife, a woman of influence.

(They kiss.)

9.

*(**KATHY** speaks out, seated. **ELLEN** sits to her left.)*

KATHY. Thank you. I wanted to speak today about tolerance. Since Ryu and I first moved here, so many of you
have welcomed us with open arms. And while I admit
that the hospitality feels wonderful, I worry that it may
be jeopardizing the authenticity of our experience –
and your own. One of the first things we learn about
the SDO is that families are brought together by the
struggle against a common obstacle. And yet, in the
effort to be neighborly, these obstacles are sometimes
neglected.

*(She looks to **ELLEN** for support, finding her footing.)*

Many of you have asked me what it's like to have an
Oriental as a husband. And I told you that Ryu is just
like you. But that isn't altogether true, is it. He isn't
like you. His eyes are a different shape. He was born in
another country, a country where suicide is noble and
gardens are made of rocks, not grass. A country that,
in the very recent past, was at war with your own. I'm
not like you either, if I would have him as my husband.

Yes, it's the North. Yes, it's 1955. There's a kind of kind-
ness born out of guilt, about the camps. But that's not
the same as tolerance, is it. We don't expect flaming
crosses on our lawn, that would be out of proportion.
But here are some ideas. You might stare at me in the
supermarket line. You might tell Ryu how much you
like Chinese food. Your teenage boys could bang trash
can lids outside our house, late at night. These are just
a few ideas.

I know, it's hard – We're all doing our best here, and I
know that we'll be able to find even more ways to give
each other an authentic experience. Thank you.

ELLEN. *(impressed)* Thank you, Kathy.
Questions for Kathy Nakata.

10.

(**KATHY** *is asleep in bed with* **RYU**, *dreaming.*)

(**ELLEN** *and* **ROGER** *sit at the foot of the bed. At least, it looks like* **ELLEN** *and* **ROGER**. *They wear '50s clothing, but they act more like* **JENNA** *and* **OMAR**.)

KATHY. Kathy still dreamed about the world she left behind.

ELLEN. *(to* **ROGER***)* So I tried the Master Cleanse?

ROGER. That's the one Beyonce did.

ELLEN. Gwyneth too.

KATHY. But tonight was different somehow...

(**KATHY** *sits up in bed. She is visibly pregnant now.*)

ELLEN. I only lasted four days.

ROGER. It gets boring right?

ELLEN. Totally. Lemon juice and cayenne, it's just like...

ROGER. *Bo*ring!

ELLEN. *Bo*ring!

ROGER. Oh hi Katha.

KATHY. "Katha."

ELLEN. Can we do anything for you?

KATHY. I – forget what I came in here for.

ELLEN. White-out, maybe?

ROGER. Or a fax sheet?

ELLEN. Maybe if you go and come back, you'll remember.

KATHY. Maybe.

(**KATHY** *starts to lie down again.*)

ROGER. *(back to* **ELLEN***)* Okay whatever. So what's going on with you. Any new suitors?

ELLEN. Well there's Ben. And there's Jerry.

ROGER. What?

ELLEN. Oh I was joking, like, "Ben and Jerry's"?

ROGER. Oh. Ha.

ELLEN. Like Saturday nights at home with a pint?

ROGER. Look on the bright side. You could have an Oriental for a husband.

ELLEN. *(delighted by the scandal)* She's *right* over *there.*

KATHY. Ryu?

(**ROGER** *and* **ELLEN** *start to exit.*)

ROGER. You could be popping out Jap babies.

ELLEN. Ohmigod, totally.

KATHY. Ryu.

ELLEN. I feel bad. Maybe I should bake her some cookies.

ROGER. You never bake *me* anything.

KATHY. Ryu!

(**RYU** *turns on a lamp and she wakes up. The others are gone now.*)

RYU. Are you okay?

KATHY. I was having a dream.

RYU. A nightmare?

KATHY. Not exactly. It was about now.

RYU. –

KATHY. I mean, the place we live now. Sort of. As opposed to where we used to live. I mean it was *about* there, but it looked like here.

RYU. *(almost asleep, humoring her)* Wow.

KATHY. Do you ever dream that way?

RYU. What way, Honey.

KATHY. About here? I mean maybe it's like moving to a foreign country. For a while, you only dream in your own language. Your sleep takes you back home. So that's the sign of real fluency – when you start dreaming in the new language.

RYU. It's four in the morning.

KATHY. Sorry. I was just / thinking.

(Sound of a brick crashing through a window.)

Oh my god.

(**RYU** *gets out of bed.*)

What was that?

(RYU goes into another room and returns with a brick in his hand.)

RYU. There's a note.

(He unwraps the paper from the brick.)

KATHY. What does it say?

RYU. *(baffled)* It's just one word.

(KATHY reads it too.)

KATHY. What does it mean?

11.

(DEAN speaks out, with ELLEN looking on.)

DEAN. Thank you all for coming. It has come to our attention that a vandal, or possibly a coordinated team of vandals, has chosen to attack the public spaces of our community.

ELLEN. And private –

DEAN. And in some cases, the private spaces too.

(Light rises on ROGER, elsewhere. He shakes a spray-paint can and starts spraying a word onto a wall. We can make out the letter "G.")

This person, or persons, is using a word designed to undermine our beloved town – And when I say undermine, I mean not only our morals and our civic beauty, but our authenticity.

(ROGER has now spray-painted the letters, "G," "O," and "O".)

This is, above all, an attack against our hard-won authenticity.

So, to the vandal, or vandals, I say, simply:

(We can make out the entire spray-painted word now: "GOOGLE.")

If this isn't the community for you, we ask you to leave peacefully at once, or face the consequences.

12.

(DEAN *and* ELLEN *arriving home.*)

ELLEN. I still don't understand, why would they paint our house and none of the others on the block?

DEAN. We're public figures, Ellen.

ELLEN. The windows of your car. The door to your office.

DEAN. Plainly we were targeted because of our position in the community.

ELLEN. You mean you. *You* were targeted.

DEAN. What are you suggesting?

ELLEN. Could it be someone you know.

Could it be –

DEAN. It could not.

(*Pause*)

(*grasping at straws*) What if it was the Communists?

ELLEN. Don't be ridiculous. This isn't about Communists.

DEAN. No, but could it be helpful if it was?

(*She looks at him.*)

The whole community is rattled. We name a few names. Possible suspects…

ELLEN. Names like who?

(*A cell phone rings. They freeze.*)

It must be an emergency.

(*It rings again – a terrible, unmistakably modern ring.*)

(DEAN *takes keys out of his pocket. He goes to a drawer. It rings again.*)

(DEAN *has opened the drawer. It rings again. He answers.*)

DEAN. Hello?

(*Light on* ROGER, *elsewhere. Maybe he's in a phone booth.*)

ROGER. I have to talk to you. I mean really talk.

(**DEAN** *tries to sound as neutral as possible.*)

DEAN. We're talking.

(*He moves a little farther from* **ELLEN**.)

ROGER. Didn't you get my messages?

DEAN. Is that what you call them?

ROGER. "Google." Our Safe Word.

(*Short pause*)

Why didn't I hear from you?

(*Pause*)

Is she there?

DEAN. Of course.

ROGER. I have to talk, like ourselves. I can't be this person any more. I feel ugly. All the time. It isn't worth it. I want to be with you. And I don't just mean fucking.

ELLEN. Who is it? /

DEAN. Headquarters.

ROGER. (*overlapping at "/"*) For a while it worked. I'm not saying it didn't.

But I wake up next to her and for the first second I'm awake I think I'm with you – and then it all comes back to me, and there's still a whole day of being someone else ahead of me.

DEAN. It's not someone else. It's you.

ROGER. If it's not someone else, why am I different in my dreams?

(*Pause.* **ELLEN** *has moved to* **DEAN**. *Touching his shoulder supportively, possessively.*)

Jason, don't hang up. Jason? I'm sick for you. I was scared that if I didn't play along… But it's worse being here and not seeing you. Or seeing you on the street and you look like you don't even know me.

That used to be hard for you too.

(*Short pause*)

ROGER. *(cont.)* What if we just walked away?

(Short pause)

It would be so easy. We could just keep walking 'til there's highways and electric signs and Toyotas. I'll go without you if I have to.

DEAN. No you won't.

ROGER. Watch me.

*(**ROGER** hangs up. His light goes out.)*

(Pause)

*(**DEAN** flips the phone shut. He puts it in his pocket, not the drawer.)*

DEAN. That was Headquarters. I have to go right away.

ELLEN. Where?

DEAN. To the city. It's an emergency.

ELLEN. What kind of emergency?

DEAN. You know I can't tell you, darling.

ELLEN. Will the community need to know?

DEAN. That's what we'll have to decide.

ELLEN. How long will you be gone this time?

DEAN. As long as it takes.

ELLEN. A day? Two days?

DEAN. As long as it takes.

ELLEN. Why don't I come with you?

DEAN. The community is unsettled. They need you –

ELLEN. They're not so unsettled. *We're* unsettled! *(Beat)* I think I should go with you.

DEAN. You know you don't make sense out there, Darling. I love that about you.

(He touches her face.)

You're my best girl.

ELLEN. I wasn't always.

(He kisses her on the cheek.)

DEAN. I better be off.

ELLEN. Why don't I make you a sandwich?

DEAN. That's all right.

ELLEN. Dean. You forgot your hat.

> *(She holds the hat out to him. The stakes seem curiously high. He goes to take the hat.)*
>
> *(He kisses her suddenly, deeply – it's meant to assuage her, but it feels like the gesture fails.)*

DEAN. Well then. *(He goes to the door.)*

I'll bring you something back. Some new fabric, maybe.

ELLEN. *(a sudden outburst)* Please don't leave me.

DEAN. I'll see you soon.

> *(And he's gone.)*

13.

*(**KATHY**, even more pregnant now, speaks to the seated circle.)*

KATHY. I don't have any answers. I'm sorry. All I know is that the Authenticity Committee has never been more necessary than it is now. Something has happened that may have changed our world forever. That word. There is simply no way to respond to it authentically. But I wonder: Why is it such an act of violence, when every one of us has it in our heads every day?

(She scans the circle for signs of unrest.)

It's impossible to forget the things we know about the world outside. It's possible, I suppose, that when you try to forget something, it can get louder and louder until all you can do is say it out loud. If that's what happened to the vandal, could it happen to you or me? How can we help each other not be…destroyed by the things we remember? I just think we need to ask the big questions.

(Pause)

I'm sorry, I know Ellen should really be leading us through this…complicated time. I'm sure she's going to be here soon. I know she would never willfully miss a meeting.

14.

*(**KATHY** is visiting **ELLEN**, who looks a wreck. Maybe she wears a robe and slippers.)*

ELLEN. Five days.

KATHY. Have you called the police?

ELLEN. It's outside their jurisdiction.

KATHY. What do you mean?

ELLEN. I mean it's...outside.

KATHY. I see.

ELLEN. He's sometimes called away like this – but never this long.

KATHY. They must really need him there.

(Pause)

Forgive me, but has it always been... happy between you two?

ELLEN. What do you mean?

KATHY. Forgive me if I'm being personal –

It's just, an attractive man like that, going off on the road...

ELLEN. You mean did he ever stray.

KATHY. Yes, thank you.

I don't mean to pry.

ELLEN. Oh Kathy, that's exactly what you mean to do.

KATHY. I'm sorry?

*(**ELLEN** lights a cigarette.)*

ELLEN. When you first moved here, we wondered if you'd mix with the community. "I don't want to be a *house-wife.*" But you've really involved yourself, Kathy. You're so *involved.* You'd think you were after my job.

KATHY. I don't think I deserve that, Ellen.

ELLEN. Oh?

KATHY. You've been locked up in this house all week, no one's seen hide nor hair of you, the girls at the Authenticity Committee are saying "Off with her head" but I stand up for you, Ellen, I say Ellen is under a lot of stress, Ellen needs our love and support right now.

ELLEN. They said "Off with her head?"

KATHY. Well, there was a little more decorum than that.

ELLEN. Look at you. You really think you can take over. And what exactly qualifies you to run a community? Is it your crab puff recipe? Or is it your miraculous fertility?

KATHY. You think I'm awfully naïve, don't you. But I know some things you don't.

ELLEN. All you know is how to keep that Jap husband of yours on a short leash.

KATHY. *Ellen.*

ELLEN. Or don't you even know that much?

Maybe that's why you're always making eyes at my husband.

KATHY. DEAN IS A HOMOSEXUAL!

(Short pause)

He and Roger. Ryu saw them together. Dean is a fucking homosexual.

(Pause. **ELLEN** *laughs to herself.)*

ELLEN. Don't you think I know that?

KATHY. What?

ELLEN. Dean and Roger have always been together.

Long before we came here, they were together.

KATHY. *(sotto voce)* Are we talking about? –

ELLEN. *(not sotto voce)* The real world, yes.

KATHY. Are you saying – what are you saying?

ELLEN. Jason and I first met in college…

KATHY. Jason?

ELLEN. Dean's real name.

We were class of '95 at Sarah Lawrence. We were room-mates the last two years. After graduation, we moved to New York together. That's when he met Roger. His first boyfriend. Roger moved in it seemed like overnight. Whenever they fought, Jason would come and talk to me. And I would listen.

KATHY. You were in love with him.

(Short pause)

ELLEN. I was in love with him.

I'm still in love with him, God help me. It's such a stupid old story, isn't it.

KATHY. It's not stupid.

ELLEN. Jason and Roger got jobs at start-ups. I got my Masters at NYU. We went to bars at night. Everything you're supposed to. But it was too easy.

KATHY. Too easy?

ELLEN. That's what Jason said. When we were trying to figure out what was wrong with us.

KATHY. So it was Jason's idea?

ELLEN. You'd press a few buttons and a tub of Häagen-Dazs would come ten minutes later. DVDs. We put the trash at the end of the hall and someone made it disappear. I took a whole class online. I got an A. There was no one watching over you, no one telling you how to live. We could do anything we wanted…so we didn't want anything. Or we didn't know what we wanted. I'm not making sense.

KATHY. No, I think I –

ELLEN. And then one day Jason met a man from a place where it was different. A man with a hat and a brief-case. Jason asked me to come with him. To be with him. He made it fun. He got down on one knee, he gave me a ring. We were laughing. Me and my gay husband. But the longer we were here, the less it was like pretend. I cooked, I cleaned, he supported me, he called me Darling – and once in a while, he would even –

KATHY. You don't have to tell me.

ELLEN. I don't see why not. He would fuck me, Kathy. Once in a while. *Quid pro quo.* But I never got pregnant, I couldn't get pregnant – like the universe knew it was pretend or something. But whenever I worried that it was all pretend, I'd look down at my ring and that was real. Even the feeling of not having a baby when everyone was supposed to be having them – that was real too, that was mine. That was something more than I had in the other world. Do you understand?

KATHY. Yes.

(ELLEN looks at her ring, touching it.)

ELLEN. It was real for Dean too.

KATHY. Of course it was.

(Pause. **ELLEN** *shakes her head, holding back tears.)*

ELLEN. The two of them, that was different. When they were together, it was like there wasn't anyone else in the world. But something went wrong. I never knew what, exactly. In the end they were always bickering, cheating on each other. Maybe they figured instead of cheating on each other, they could cheat *with* each other. Or if they had to hide, it would make things more –

(a sudden break) I'm tired of seeing it from his perspective.

KATHY. Of course.

ELLEN. Dean carried out his homosexuality in a perfectly authentic way, with the right shame and secrecy. Of course I saw the clues – he'd say he couldn't sleep, he'd go out for night walks... And I'd suspect, the way a '50s wife would suspect. And I'd be grateful that I was the one he came home to. And it was harder than our old life, and it was better.

(Pause)

KATHY. But, if you already knew about Dean, then why are you...

ELLEN. Such a fucking mess?

KATHY *(as in "I wasn't going to say it")* Well.

ELLEN. Because I know he isn't coming back this time. *(with sudden difficulty)*
What am I going to do?

KATHY. I'm going to speak firmly for a moment, Ellen.
You have to bury your husband. You have to fit this into your Dossier.

ELLEN. −

KATHY. The key will be to make everything as true as possible.

ELLEN. How?

KATHY. Maybe we say that Dean and Roger *were* homosexuals, yes. They both had wonderful wives, but their deepest desires were eating at them from the inside.

ELLEN. But Dean, no one will believe that he would / just leave his −

KATHY. *(placating)* We'll say that Dean rejected that part of himself. He cut things off with Roger, he prayed, he…killed the darkness in himself. But Roger couldn't accept it. That's why he started terrorizing the community.
Finally he asked Dean to meet him in a park one night. And, when Dean rejected him again…Roger shot him.

ELLEN. And himself. He killed himself too.

KATHY. Good.

(Beat)

The official story will be a little different, of course: We'll call it a mugging, maybe…a tragic mugging. Dean couldn't sleep, he was out for one of his night walks, maybe he ran into a vagrant.

(Short pause)

We'll buy you a widow's dress. We'll have a beautiful funeral. Dean was so important to this community.

ELLEN. And I'm supposed to just…be that forever? The widow everyone's sorry for?

KATHY. Or you could leave.

(They lock eyes.)

But think how rich it will be. How complicated. When you pass by, people will whisper, why was Dean in that particular park, so far from his house? Some people might even whisper that he ran off to be a homosexual in that other world. People will whisper. What could be more authentic than that?

But everyone will be so moved by how you handle it. With your head held high and proud through all the gossip.

ELLEN. Yes.

KATHY. And when you're ready, you'll come back to the committee.

(Short pause)

ELLEN. What about his responsibilities? Dean did more in that job than anyone knows.

KATHY. Just leave that to me.

ELLEN. You're being so nice to me. Why do you even want me to stay?

KATHY. Because you're my neighbor. *(Beat)*

You've been so helpful to me, Ellen. I'm so happy I can help you now.

15.

(RYU speaks out. KATHY stands farther off, enormously pregnant now.)

RYU. First of all, welcome. Welcome to the SDO.

I'm sure you all have a lot of questions.

"What do I wear?"

"How do I talk?"

"How do I explain this to the kids?"

Kathy and I will help you answer all of these perfectly normal questions.

KATHY. The most important thing to remember is that all of us were newcomers at one point. I mean gosh, we're *still* newcomers. Ryu and I have only been here, what

RYU. Fourteen months.

KATHY. Fourteen months. And Ryu's already the floor manager at the box factory. I'm so proud.

RYU. Honey...

KATHY. Now I'm embarrassing him, but I think it's important to know how life in 1955 can really focus you.

In the modern world, people are always talking about their problems. Always asking "How can I be happier?" Maybe if I had a different diet, maybe if I had a different therapist. A different childhood. In the '50s, you have to keep it together. You aren't just living for yourself. You have a responsibility to make life wonderful for your husband and your child – and your community. *(suddenly more personal)* It's amazing how...healing that responsibility can be.

(RYU comes forward to join KATHY.)

RYU. We are not saying life is better in the 1950s. We are not saying people are happier necessarily. We are saying that they're more *present*.

KATHY. Thank you, yes.

RYU. We are not in pursuit of the past.

We are in pursuit of the present.

(The baby kicks inside **KATHY**.*)*

KATHY. Oh.

RYU. What is it?

KATHY. *(hand to her belly)* The present.

16.

*(***KATHY*** *is asleep next to ***RYU****, dreaming.)*

*(***DEAN*** *and ***ELLEN*** *in the living room, still dressed in '50s clothing.)*

KATHY. Kathy hardly ever dreamed of that other world any more. Most nights she dreamed a row of houses just like the ones at Maple and Vine.

DEAN. It was a lovely day, wasn't it.

ELLEN. It was. One of the loveliest I can remember.

DEAN. I'm a little hungry. Are you hungry, Darling?

ELLEN. Yes, a bit. I suppose I should get dinner on the table.

KATHY. But tonight her dream was different.
    In this dream, everything was a little bit easier.

ELLEN. Were you thinking of something in particular?

DEAN. Oh anything, really. Whatever you can whip up.

KATHY. In this world, there was a button to call for everything.

*(The doorbell rings. ***ELLEN*** opens the door and there is an entire Thanksgiving dinner sitting on the welcome mat.)*

DEAN. That looks wonderful, Honey.

ELLEN. Thank you.

KATHY. There was a button for bringing the milk, and a button for crab puffs, and a button for soggy cake, God knows why.

*(***DEAN*** examines the turkey.)*

DEAN. It smells delicious.

ELLEN. It does, doesn't it.

(The doorbell rings again.)

Who could that be now?

KATHY. There was even a button for bringing the things you most desire, so you didn't have to go looking for them in the night.

(**ELLEN** *opens the door and* **ROGER** *is there. He looks at* **DEAN**.)

DEAN. Well, what are you waiting for? Come on in.

ELLEN. Are you hungry, Roger?

ROGER. *(looking at* **DEAN***)* Always.

KATHY. All of these buttons were part of a brand-new machine. And the genius of this machine was that it brought things to people, instead of bringing people to things.

ELLEN. I'll put a record on. It's so much nicer to eat with music.

DEAN. Something slow and pretty.

(**ELLEN** *doesn't lift a finger, but light rises on the hi-fi. A beautiful piece of night music starts to play.*)

ROGER. What is that? Brahms?

ELLEN. *(there is no album cover)* I'm not sure, the album cover just says "Classical for Lovers."

KATHY. This worked with information too – so there was no more need to go to a library to learn the answer to something. Now you only had to wonder for a few moments.

DEAN. It's Chopin. The "Raindrop Prelude."

ROGER. Ah yes.

ELLEN. You could almost dance to it.

KATHY. And before long, there was no more need to go anywhere.

(**ROGER** *holds out his hand to* **DEAN**.)

ROGER. Well?

DEAN. I have two left feet.

ROGER. *(gentle)* I know.

KATHY. There was no longer anyone watching over you. No one to tell you what you could or couldn't do.

(**DEAN** *takes* **ROGER**'s *hand. They start to slow dance to the music, very simply and beautifully.*)

The new machinery worked so smoothly that people never sensed how it was changing them.

(**ELLEN** *watches them dancing while she eats. Content. The dream doesn't get scarier exactly, so much as it gets more hypnotically tranquil, more enveloping.*)

These warm and well-fed people didn't realize that they were dying inside.

(**RYU** *stirs in bed.*)

RYU. Kath.

KATHY. It was so easy to get what they wanted that they no longer wanted anything.

(**DEAN** *and* **ROGER** *come apart. The dream starts to fade away.*)

RYU. Kathy.

KATHY. It was so long since they'd had to go anywhere or talk to anyone, that they forgot who they even were. They thought they knew, but somehow, slowly, they'd forgotten.

RYU. Kathy.

(**RYU** *touches her and she wakes up. The music goes out.*)

KATHY. What?

(*The others are gone now.*)

RYU. It's okay. You were talking in your sleep.

KATHY. What was I saying?

RYU. I couldn't make it out. But you sounded scared.

KATHY. I was having a dream.

RYU. A nightmare?

KATHY. Yes.

RYU. Well you're okay now.

(We hear the soft crying of a baby in a crib next to the bed. **RYU** *picks up the baby.)*

Shhh. Shhh.

(He hands **KATHY** *the baby.)*

We're here at Maple and Vine, and your daughter is almost sleeping through the night.

(He holds **KATHY** *as she rocks the baby.)*

RYU. It was all a bad dream.

KATHY. Yes.

Yes it was, wasn't it.

End of Play

Also by
Jordan Harrison...

Amazons and Their Men

Doris to Darlene

Fit for Feet

Lightning Source UK Ltd.
Milton Keynes UK
UKOW06f1502100816

280347UK00001B/16/P

9 780573 700217